From Our Eyes and Ears:

Writings by Musicians of Color
Volume 1: Black Voices

Edited by

Lorin Green & LaVonna Wright

AQUARIUS PRESS
Detroit, Michigan

From Our Eyes & Ears:
Writings by Musicians of Color, Volume 1: Black Voices

Cover design: Lorin Green and LaVonna Wright

ISBN 978-1-7330898-6-9
LCCN 2024937837

AQUARIUS PRESS
www.AquariusPress.net

Printed in the United States of America

This volume of the anthology is dedicated to my late grandmother,
Annie Mae Paige-Bell;
a most loved and missed pillar within my family.
You are always near.

Volume 1

Contents

Preface

"Oh, are you new here? Let me guess: JazzVocalist?"

"You speak really well."

"When I think of a flute player, I don't think of a Black girl."

Microaggressions have been a significant part of my life and the lives of many if not all other minorities that are within the western classical music field. Not allowing myself to show any response to these words has become something that is as effortless as breathing. I know there are not many people who look like me in my field. When I was a child, this made me wonder if Black people just didn't do classical music, or worse, if Black people didn't belong in classical music. My ancestors were brought over on ships; beaten, whipped, starved, killed for the privilege and purpose of those who saw themselves as their superior. Why are my people still excluded from certain fields in this country that has a lot to make up for in terms of reparations? Is classical music one of the many pillars of white supremacy that still linger in this country? If so, I will be a part of seeing it fall.

Acknowledgments

There have been countless people who have entered my life and who have inspired me to pursue this project. To all the friends and mentors who have guided me throughout the creation of this anthology, thank you. I could not have done this without the work, time, and dedication given by one of my dearest friends and brilliant mind LaVonna Wright, and all the contributors of this anthology. It could not have been done without you all.

Thank you to my mother, Sherie Bell, for your endless prayers and love. Thank you to my brother, Stephen, for always being there.

To everyone who has inspired me and supported me in anyway, this is for you.

—Lorin Green

Editor's Note

Dear Reader,

We invite you to read this anthology of writings that shines light on the prejudice, stigmas, and stereotypes facing musicians of color in the western classical music field. This first volume features selections by musicians of Black descent, illuminating Black voices in the field.

The content throughout this work may shock you, sadden you, and inspire you to take action. Ultimately, these works share only a face to the inequities and trauma that span across creative fields. As such,these pieces will present covert and overt examples of racism, such as language, that may be upsetting or triggering.

We honor all of the contributors who were brave enough to share their stories: thank you once more for your exceptional work, here and in the western classical music field. The end of the anthology provides a section, "About the Contributors." Feel free to reach out and thank or connect with a contributor.

We look forward to making these stories known and heard, from our eyes and ears.

—LaVonna Wright, MA

Introduction

The field of western classical music has continued to be a field that is Eurocentric in more than one domain. According to a nationwide study conducted by the League of American Orchestras between 1980 and 2014 and published in 2016, the professional orchestral field remains to be occupied majorly by white males with African Americans making up an average of 1.8% of orchestras nationwide, Hispanics making up 2.5%, and Asian/Pacific Islanders being over 9% by 2014.I conducted an experiment where I asked collegiate music students to name the first three composers that came to their mind. The answers were a variation of "Bach, Beethoven, Stravinsky, Bartok,Tchaikovsky" etc. I asked if anyone had noticed a pattern: no one did. I then asked everyone to name three female composers. Only one could name three and the majority could only name one. I then went on to ask everyone to name three composers of color and then specifically three Black female and male composers. You can imagine how sparse those responses were. The purpose of the experiment was not to shame anyone for their lack of knowledge in regard to minority composers but to expose the system in which western classically trained musicians are subject to.

As a Black woman within the western classical music field, I am being topical when I say that I do not see people who look like me represented well within my field. And for those within the field who do look like me, the road is almost never easy. We have seen instances where musicians of color at the top of their fields deal with situations of racial tension. Many of these musicians will also comment on how they had to work 10 times harder than their non-POC colleagues to be in the same place they are. I recall a conversation with a friend where they mentioned that they could never be just as good as everyone else in the room but they in fact had to be better than everyone in the room to be considered their equal. I have also been present in situations where musicians of color have been challenged and had their quality of musicianship questioned within ensembles more than anyone else. Why do minorities have to prove that we belong in these spaces time and time again, and why do we have to work so much harder than our white colleagues to be considered at the same level?

Nothing that I have said is new, groundbreaking information for anyone who is aware of the racial state of the western classical music field. Many are aware of the lack of representation of minorities within our field, and there have been numerous organizations and initiatives created to battle this problem. So why are we not seeing an exponential increase in not only representation of minorities within the western classical music field but also equitable practices that would encourage more minorities to pursue a career in music? The phrase "pull the rug up" is one that I have found myself referencing more often these days. The phrase's meaning is that in order to know you have a problem, you must expose the problem, and by doing this we are then able to fix the problem.

Kimberlé Williams Crenshaw is a pioneer in critical race theory and addresses this idea in her 2016 Ted Talk "The Urgency of Intersectionality". She shares an instance where

Emma DeGraffenreid, a Black woman, felt as if she was not given a job opportunity due to the fact that she was a Black woman, and her case was dismissed on the grounds that the company that she had applied for had hired Black in the past. What Emma was trying to imply was that it was not only the fact that she was Black that she felt as if she wasn't given the job opportunity, but the fact that she was a Black woman. The oversight occurred due to the fact that the lack of representation by Black women was not seen as a problem therefore the problem would not be fixed. Pulling the rug up allows for situations to be solved, and the creation of this anthology is my way of pulling the rug up.

There are numerous sources that confront and address the problems of diversity, equity, and inclusion within the field of western classical music. Many of these sources unmask these problems through factual and statistical evidence and often give solutions to these problems or show what has been done to combat these problems. I have found that it is not statistics or factual evidence that often changes viewpoints and mindsets, but it is often personal stories and connections that bring about changes of opinion. During the spring and early summer of 2020 when there was a wave of racial tension within our nation, some took it upon themselves to share stories of situations that they had to endure due to their race. I took this as an opportunity to share personal stories and situations that I had gone through due to me being an Black woman within my field of classical music. I was very surprised by the number of responses that I received including other minorities who had gone through similar situations and non-POC who spoke of their lack of awareness of the racial situation within our field. This showed me that not everyone within our field understands that there is a racial situation, or rather not everyone realizes how prominent the situation really is. More than anything this showed me how personal stories were the key to awareness and that awareness is what could spark the change that we want to see in regard to diversity, inclusion, and most importantly equity within our field.

Played Like an Instrument, Fought Like an Animal

Marcel Benoit III

Since the first slave ship landed on American soil, Black people have been imposed with needing a purpose. For Black people, there is no opportunity for us to just exist. Only to be used as some sort of pawn in a predominately white world. This concept has infiltrated our community and has manifested as generational trauma for many BIPOC, thus affecting our roles as musicians.

Particularly in America, Black people have pioneered the most prevalent genres of music such as jazz, the blues, rap & hip-hop, etc. Yet, we are treated as tokens in most professional and academic musical spaces. Black people are expected to respect the musical accomplishments of white cis men but are discouraged from pursuing formal research on topics that celebrate Blackness. In my lifetime, I have felt the sting of racism and disrespect from microaggressions to deliberate ignorant actions against me. I hope that these stories elucidate the internal and external struggle of navigating a career as a Black musician.

Unsolicited

When I was a sophomore in high school, I had already made a bit of a name for myself as one of the better singers in school. I was in the advanced chorus, I performed with the All-State choirs, and I was a part of nearly every theatrical production, particularly the musicals. As such, most of what I did with my days had to do with me singing, even if I did not want to. In my English class, there was a week where my teacher felt she needed to discuss something with the class regarding something she had seen. She explained to us that while she was monitoring the hallway, she noticed a group of students and overheard their conversation. The group consisted of mostly Black students and one white student and she hears the white student use the word, "nigga." When recounting the story, she used that word in its entirety seemingly with no remorse. As a woman who was both white and blonde, she felt very affected by the student's use of the word and repeated it several times. This sparked a whole week of impromptu focus on Black history and Black literature. In theory, this sounds like a progressive and enriching opportunity for my predominantly white English class.

However, it was an opportunity to alienate and exploit the knowledge of the few Black students in my class. During each class, she would ask a Black student to explain or demonstrate something of importance to Black culture rather than researching the information herself because she felt that it was inappropriate for her to explain these concepts. She felt that repeating a polarizing racial slur to spark discussion was the extent of her abilities as an educator. During one class that week, she asked me to stand up and sing either a slave song or a negro spiritual. I explained to her that I did not want to and she implored me to just sing anyway because she felt that it would be better than listening to some "old recording." To escape this situation, I said that I didn't know any songs to sing right now. She told me that if I wanted, I could learn a song outside of class, for no extra credit, and perform for the class next time. She then explained that maybe if I sing for her, then she will invite the principal to class to hear it and that I could be a famous gospel singer someday. At that moment, she created a life plan for me that I expressed no interest in and wanted me to make this decision on the spot. I noticed her eyes light up when she came up with the idea of "helping" me this way. I believe she thought that I was looking for my "big break" and that I needed someone like her to get there. I realized that she did not know me, she just knew what I looked like. She knew that I was Black and she knew that I sing. She assumed that all I want to do with my life is sing slave songs. Her altruism allowed me to be privy to her true colors.

You Should Just Do It

As a college student, I was a lot more secure in myself and particularly more secure as a Black person. I majored in choral music education because I have a yearning to teach the art of singing and I am inspired by musical academics. My inspiration grew a bit thin as I realized that even the most accomplished minds in a liberal field are very familiar with generalizing based on race.

When it came to performing, I wanted to exercise my ability to sing classically, chorally, and in an operatic setting. I am open to all types of singing, but classical training was my raison d'être. For the most part, I was able to express myself musically in a way that best suited my talents. However, during a choir rehearsal,we concluded that asking me to "rap" during a song was our best bet. While performing with the men's choir, we decided to sing a choral arrangement of a pop song that included a rap. What is more is that it was a rap about racial inequality referring to the historic marches that took place in Selma, Alabama. I have never marketed myself as a rapper or as someone well-versed in hip-hop. While I did not want to perform the rap, I felt obligated to say yes as there were only two or three Black singers in the men's choir and I certainly did not want there to be an opportunity for someone to perform in a way that was disrespectful or ignorant to our message. I agreed to perform, but I decided to go the alternative route of performing the spoken word instead of the rap. During rehearsals for the performance, I often stammered on my words or fell out of the rhythm of my speech. I was dealing with the inner conflict of performing this earnestly yet poignant without becoming a caricature of a Black person. My white colleagues wanted to offer me advice on how to perform the spoken word with the passion that my director wanted. They all alluded to mimicking famous African American activists or copying the syntax and speech patterns of characters from tv shows who are Black. I was already disappointed that I let myself be put in this situation. While my director felt that she was giving me a voice, I felt silenced. There is always some template that society places on Black people and we get vilified if we try to do anything different.

On the day of the performance, I was nervous and I made a couple of mistakes in my spoken word. The predominantly white audience met me with awe while saying empty platitudes to make up for what felt like a lie. "I was so moved by your words!""Your speech was so inspiring!" "Such a powerful performance." Their kind words felt like salt on the wound as I was dealing with small details that made this one of the lowlights of my career.

Do The Song Justice

Making a living as a musician comes with its obstacles and being a Black musician gives higher hurdles to clear. While I was in college, I also started working as a singer for a second source of income. A few weeks after the start of my second semester in college, I found work as a choral scholar at a predominantly white episcopal church. The organization of their worship services was a bit of a culture shock for me, but it was easy to get used to. What proved to be more difficult was having an identity other than being a Blackman. I am proud of my culture and my heritage, but I see no necessity in reminding a Black person that they are Black. During my three-and-a-half years performing with the church choir, I constantly found myself having to explain my background to people. There were many probing questions about whether I knew my immediate family, if I knew how to read music, if I was a jazz performer or not, asking me what kind of performing I wanted to do.

Despite the fact every other choral scholar was a music education major, no one assumed the same for me. They thought I wanted to be a pop singer or a gospel singer and had little knowledge of motets, anthems, or any sacred music for that matter. For Christmas, some members of the church choir thought it would be nice to get the choral scholars some gifts. Each scholar received a gift based on interests they had expressed at some point. However, when it came to my gift, I received a songbook of famous Negro Spirituals. The person who gave it to me told me that she wanted me to sing one of the songs for her one day and explained that she has been waiting to meet someone who could "do the song justice." I accepted her gift, knowing that she meant no harm by her words, but the experience stuck with me because I realized that she sees me as a 'Black person' and not a 'person who is Black.' This sentiment is shared with a member of the congregation from this church who felt it was her mission to seek me out before and after church services. She was enamored with me. She said that she loved my voice and that she comes to other services just to hear me sing. I was flattered by this and I enjoyed talking with her until she made a certain remark at me. She invited one other friend who was an assistant principal of a local middle school. She wanted us to meet so I could make an impression on him and maybe he would hire me as a choir teacher at his school.

He explained that he liked my singing and thought I would be a great fit for a choir position, but they had no open jobs for teaching chorus. He said that there was an opening for a band teacher and I joked that I would not be the best candidate for that. However, before I was able to finish my sentence, she told him that it would be better if I just took the job away from the current choir teacher because I am a Black boy and it would look good for both of us. I cannot remember what my face was expressing at that moment, but fortunately, I had to leave shortly after she made that comment. Whenever anyone makes comments like that, it proves to me that race is typically a small issue for white people amongst themselves. She passively commented that my Blackness can be exploited for social recognition and would receive a job in exchange. She continued to try and strike up a conversation with me for the remainder of my time there. I do not believe she regrets making that comment and will probably find another Black person to help her fulfill her white savior complex. I hope that the next person she clings onto like that will be smarter than me and make more of an effort to avoid her.

These examples are only a glimpse into the myriad of times that my musicianship was put into question. They represent what many Black people experience as musicians in a white-dominated society and shed some light on why there may be apprehension from BIPOC to perform in white spaces. The emotional toll it takes is overwhelming; at times as it directly affects how I operate as a singer.

I find myself questioning whether I am paying homage to my people or if I am staying true to myself. These experiences force me to reevaluate my identity everywhere I go. I think of how much easier it would be to go about my life knowing that people see me as my accomplishments or my actions and not by the shade of my skin or the texture of my hair.

We Have to Talk

Jessica Bell

There are many layers to being Black within the arts. I look at it as a multi-dimensional lifestyle. For instance, many of us code-switch through many spaces in our everyday lives, but being a musician means code-switching times ten. Many times, when we are in spaces we condense to our smallest selves. I, for one, have done so many times and that has played a part in me not being as confident as I should be when I perform. Working through these insecurities would have to be one of the most challenging things that I've done throughout my entire musical career. I realize that many of these insecurities aren't mine after all. Once I realized this, my confidence developed into something completely different—something I've never felt before. I think it's very important that as Black musicians we know that sometimes spaces are not inclusive or not diverse but that does not mean that we dim our lights. That does not mean that you can't be confident in what it is that you do. The most difficult part of navigating these spaces is looking at the art form that you're studying and seeing that in most cases, the curriculum is telling you that *every part of your existence is wrong.*

Working through this and creating spaces that include not only you, your voice, and your talent, but include spaces for others like you is the most rewarding part of it all. Sometimes being in these white spaces forces you to go into the shadows. Either you're looked at as not good enough or fit enough for this art form, or you're tokenized.

As I discussed with Philip Ewell, professor of music theory at Hunter College and the CUNY Graduate Center, some of the curricula, whether it be music theory or music history, is fundamentally racist. I remember going to some of these classes and just thinking to myself, "Wow this does not relate to me at all." I remember skipping Music History because I was tired of learning about a new version of the same story—another white man from a different country that cheated, killed someone, and it goes on and on the same way each time. The framework in which we look at Music History is flawed. We're taking music history and framing it in Western Europe and only focusing on this new version of classical music.

What happened to every other country? What were their musical contributions?

How can we focus on western classical music without focusing on the influences of the slave trade?

Seriously, ask yourself how we could talk about music history and the creation of pianos and all of these instruments without talking about slavery.

Who were the laborers?

Where did these materials come from? Who invented these instruments?

We have to talk about the origin of instruments, the origins of instrument parts. We have to talk about the origin of languages. All of these historical events play an intricate part in western classical music and the formation of any music. This made me question what I'm really learning. If I were a white male who had always known white western classical music it would be unconsciously programming me to be racist. I say this with a grain of salt because I don't think that the curriculum is blatantly racist, meaning it consciously excludes the Black musician, artist, or laborer from the story. The way that the curriculum is taught is actually doing even more damage by subliminally programming students to believe that this white male framework of music is "right". I felt the smallest going to these classes knowing that it was going to be another one of the same stories that didn't include me.

Being a Black musician isn't always bad. There are many positives to the space as well. My favorite part about being a Black musician is creating art with other Black musicians and artists. It is the most warming and relatable thing that I've done in my entire career. Another one is automatically being diverse and having a different perspective than most ofyour peers. Being a Black musician is fun, simply put. I feel honored to be able to be in the position that I am in to create music and be a part of this because of artists that came beforeme.I aspire to be like so many Black musicians and I aspire to inspire others. All in all, I think that it is trivial for us to constantly have to prove ourselves and decipher between a good or bad Black musician. We should exist ino ur art and creativity, simply put. My hope for musical spaces moving forward is to include a more diverse framework for curriculum. Ifwe start here, then the behaviors will slowly but eventually follow.

Only One in the Room

A Conversation With Dr. Tonya Mitchell-Spradlin

Lorin: What brought you to conducting?

Tonya: I suppose you could say that conducting was a natural part of my progression as a music educator. From playing the clarinet in the sixth-grade band, I knew I wanted to be a band director. I absolutely loved putting my instrument together while being near my friends, accomplishing new challenges, and forcing my brain to multitask. I also loved being part of a team activity with as hared goal. I knew I wanted a future helping to shape that type of environment. Between lessons, youth bands and orchestras, honor bands and All states, and finally music school, my desire to form musical environments never changed. Though I grew up with a single mother of three, I feel very privileged that she prioritized our activities and hobbies making sure she could take my two brothers and I to all our events and attend as many as possible. My mother drove me from Lawrenceville, Georgia to Bloomington, Indiana when I auditioned for the music school at IU, and continued to make the nine-hourdrivefororientation, move-in , and even a couple of football games when I became drum major. She also supported me in my first job as Director of Bands at Chamblee High School in Chamblee, GA by coming to all my band concerts. A career in music can be a difficult choice for some—especially now following the pandemic. I am fortunate to have grown up in an environment that allowed my passion to flourish.

Lorin: Were there any situations that occurred during any point of your education that really shaped how you saw your path within your career?

Tonya: Shifting from teaching public school, in my case high school, to teaching college shifted my perspective on my personal role in band. I've always been very purpose driven and goal oriented. While teaching public school I felt I was making an immediate impact and difference in my students' lives. I saw them multiple hours a day, engaged with them before and after school, and taught many of them for 2-3 class periods a day between multiple concert bands, jazz band, AP Music Theory, and marching band after school (oh and I also coached track for two years!). I was involved in so much more of their lives than just teaching music. I truly felt like part of the community, part of their village. For many students, I could literally see the moment when their stress faded away from other classes/activities and their enjoyment and comfort kicked in. I craved those moments. My mission was to grow the person through music, to instill deep understanding of musical concepts so that they could make informed decisions about phrasing, balance, blend, and personal and group growth. That is still my goal; however, the setting looks very different. I learned very quickly that when conducting a collegiate wind ensemble, time is limited, and therefore you have to get more creative with establishing bonds in a shorter period of time. It's a value system of mine to form connections with my students, it is also difficult to do that in seven to eleven two-hour rehearsals while also needing to prepare for a concert. At first, I found it difficult to merge preparation with getting to know students. I've since gotten much better at it over the years.

In those years I noticed the biggest factor that has shaped my realization of my role in this sphere: the higher up I move in my profession, the less diverse it gets. As a Black woman, I've gotten very used to being the only one in the room. This was not something I experienced until college and not something that started to bother me until I began teaching at the collegiate level. Perhaps this is because I happened to grow up and teach high school in an extremely diverse area outside of Atlanta, Georgia. Teaching collegiately, I often felt out of place, looked down on, underestimated, or simply left out. Those feelings are a mixture of actual and perceived feelings. I noticed that the more "clout" I gained, the less diverse my students were, my colleagues were, the curriculum was. I would say around 2017-2018 is where I felt the biggest "what is my purpose here?" crisis. Gone were the days ofmolding young 14-year-olds still figuring out their lives but loving the release and challenge of band. Now I'm helping to mold young 20-somethings still figuring out their lives but loving the release and challenge of band! The big difference is that the 20 somethings have chosen to embark on a path of music making for a living. Therefore,my purpose became deeply and boldly invested in the type of teacher and musician I would want to see in the world: one that is exceptionally knowledgeable, hardworking, empathetic, inquisitive, open minded, and aware of spaces where they can make meaningful change. Most first year teachers start their first jobs armed with the knowledge they learned from school; therefore, I find it critical to expose them to as much as I can. In my sphere, I get to do this through my programming, my repertoire, my guest artist visits, my curriculum, my conversations, our tours, etc… I actively work towards multi-demographic concerts in terms of the composers represented, the styles presented, even the concert experience itself—there is generally a multi-media element (use of screens, technology, other mediums,etc…) We have open discussions on the meaning of the music we play, we ingest, and how we do so. I feel that by doing the latter which is so much more than just preparing a concert program, I am achieving my vision for what an educator and life shaper should be.

Have you faced any challenges within your fields of conducting and music education and have you ever experienced imposter syndrome? If so, how do you deal with it?

I have faced several challenges in a variety of forms in my career. Some have been externally induced and some internal struggles. These struggles have caused feelings of imposter syndrome often. It is something I feel less and less as I continue through my career, but I am unsure if it will ever fully go away.

One challenge I actively focus on is balance. For creatives, and all music teachers are creatives, there is no limit to how much "work" can go into a single project. Between concert programming, score study, rehearsals, rehearsal review, media, recruitment, sharing events, networking, collaborating, and thinking ahead to future projects, it's very easy to extend planning outside of"normal" work hours. There is a perception in our field that being the first to arrive and last to leave or extending hours into the evenings or weekends is the definition of hard work. Though there are situations where the latter is unavoidable (marching band, extracurriculars, etc...) I've learned that setting boundaries has helped me with the challenge of balance. Recently, I have begun to prioritize and protect my weekends, evenings, and holidays. Instead of immediately saying "yes" to requests, I assess whether I can truly fit something into my schedule even if my calendar says I'm open. For instance, when agreeing to a 2-day guest appearance, we often spend hours programming, arranging seating charts, and communicating with the site hosts. Additionally, though the event may only be 2-days, depending on where one lives, an entire day of travel is needed before and after, necessitating missing work and family events. I have begun to put limits on my travel to ensure I'm prioritizing my home and family in addition to my career. As a woman expecting her first child, this has become increasingly important to me. I am finding that I have to say no more frequently, set my schedule years in advance (yes years), and actively build in family time in my schedule. My younger self simply assumed I would fit it in between work; however, I was finding that my work would expand to fit all times I allowed it. Therefore, I find it works for me to design my schedule with personal time, family time, and work combined.

Another challenge I've faced is often being the only Black woman in a room. I'm sure much of imposter syndrome has stemmed from feeling otherized in situations where I don't see myself reflected. There have been very few instances ofobvious and direct sexism or racism that I've encountered in my career; however, I notice microaggressions, indirect slights, and isolation on a small scale often. I have served on several committees where it has been clear that my presence was to be seen not heard, therefore making all of my contributions seemingly unwanted. Despite working exceptionally hard and maintaining a national presence, I've had directors or colleagues only address my appearance instead of my work output. I've been kept out of conversations, decisions, and important actions. I've experienced giving great ideas, only to have them shot down but praised when a male colleague suggested the same thing. I tend to notice these events more now than ever before because of my position putting me in places where important decisions are being made. I think a lot of change is happening and as a whole our community is doing a better job of recognizing these issues; however, as with all things in academia, they are slow to change and often require a "first" to use their voice to help instill that change for those to follow.

There are a few tools I use to overcome challenges. One is extreme organization. Large tasks become considerably more manageable when broken down into smaller parts. I find that when I outline the steps needed to accomplish a task by writing them down, I am more productive, focused, and can ensure all steps align with the overall goal. It also keeps my mind from spinning out of control!

With all things difficult I like to think of Glennon Doyle's quote from the book *Untamed*, "We can do hard things." I also remind myself that rest is not synonymous with weakness.

What work have you done in terms of diversity, inclusion, and equity within your fields?

The most notable work I've done as a champion for DEI, balance, and access is to center that value system at the heart of my programs and philosophy. All action begins with purpose. I have made it my purpose to be as inclusive as possible in all aspects within my sphere of influence. In regard to programming, all programs contain styles, time periods, and composer backgrounds representing a wide variety of demographics. This is true for programs at Penn State and for honor bands/guest appearances. In my time at Penn State, I've partnered with the composition studio to perform works of student composers, local composers, and engage with guests in order to feature new voices. In bringing in guests, my focus is always to expose my students to engaging, interesting, exceptional music—this has manifested itself in a wide range of personalities, backgrounds, demographics, and experiences. As a member of the Association of Black Women Band Directors I am engaged in lifting the voices of other Black female conductors. Additionally, I've held many service positions including editor of new music for the Women Band Directors International journal and National Vice President of Professional Relations for Tau Beta Sigma that have allowed me to showcase voices that add variety to the Eurocentric male musical tradition. I still don't feel like I'm doing enough. This year my focus is to take my ensembles outside the walls of Penn State and bring our ensembles to communities that may not be able to engage with us regularly. I intend to visit more schools where resources are slim and where students don't often see women of color in spaces like mine.

What changes do you hope to see within our field in the near and distant future?

I hope to see our field taking an active role in bringing music to schools, to communities, to areas that may not know the wonderful sounds that a wind ensemble creates. I feel we too often sit and wait for people to come to us; however, it's a small group of people who have the time to attend singular Tuesday evening ticketed concerts in a location that may be difficult to access.

I hope that we start to value mental health in our profession. The "go go go, sleep when you're dead" mentality is causing extreme burnout and turning an already exhausting field into an unmanageable one for many teachers. I have often felt and even been told that it's okay to take free time for myself once I've reached a certain standard or position. While still an advocate for hard work, I hope we can infuse our next generation with a balance that allows for high-achieving accomplishments as well as true rest and recovery.

Finally, I hope that we see so much diversity that we can stop talking about the need for diversity. My hope is that if it is a value system and part of our philosophy just as much as choosing dynamic repertoire, making efficient lesson plans, etc… we can simply see a more diverse landscape. For many, being inclusive is still thought of as something extra to do after the primary planning is concluded. I hope that this important idea is simply embedded in our daily practices.

Bold of You to Assume

Camille Core

Close your eyes.

Imagine that you are 13 years old.

Your entire life, you are surrounded by minorities and people who look just like you. You have yet to have a teacher who was not a POC. You are completely uprooted in the middle of your prime middle school life, just after you comfortably assimilated. You become the new student,in a new state, in the eighth grade and you are HORRIFIED! While attending the Open House, you have one chance to get somewhat acquainted with the school before you officially start. Overwhelmed by all the "newness," you find a safe haven: a chorus information table presents itself in the most angelic way possible. Seeing this as the ultimate sign, you walk over and see a kind, middle-aged white woman who warmly greets you with a smile. You explain to her that you have just moved and that this is something you are very interested in. She then pops your recently inflated bubble by asking, "do you sing a lot of R&B and listen to a lot of hip hop?" At that moment, it does not seem like that big of a deal, so you answer the question. However, after processing this, you realize that this question was rooted in a bold generalization.

Now open your eyes.

I know, BOLD OF HER TO ASSUME!!! I hate to say it, but this was definitely a "because you're Black" moment. She assumed that "because I'm Black" I must love the forms of music that are still heavily dominated by Black artists. This was my first encounter with micro-aggressions. As previously mentioned, I did not realize the micro-aggression at the time, so I remained in choir.

Nonetheless, this experience remained with me throughout that school year and still does to this day. I felt confused, hurt, and slightly discouraged. From that day forward, I made it a point to emphasize my enjoyment of other styles of music and that is something I should not have to do. If I say I am a musician, the only assumption that should be made is that I am a lover of the art form of music and music making, with no barrier on genre. Let this story be a lesson, especially if you are a current or future educator, the world of music is too vast for you to make such a bold assumption.

Among Us

Lauryn Davis

I was talking to my good friend.

She has been saying that she has been suffering with Imposter Syndrome and it developed during her time in undergrad. This made me rethink about how other people, specifically non-POC who are supposed to be "professionals," can really affect our mental space and self-esteem as Black people. We already carry a lot of trauma as it is and attempting to create a name for ourselves in a predominately white genre of music is a tough area to navigate. In the final spring semester at my institution, I had to put on a Senior Recital. Three weeks before the recital, there is a permission jury—mind you, I have seen plenty of classmates who never rise to the occasion of singing pass their permission jury. However, there was one out of the thirteen pieces that were "not up to par" per "their standards" and they proceeded to make me redo those certain pieces. Once this happened, it made me feel a certain way because my counterparts never endured as much push-back as I did. I am truly aware of having standards and expectations; However, everyone should be held to the same standards and expectations.

The way these professionals pick and choose when to uphold "their standards" gave me a glimpse of how the imposter syndrome begins. People will try to control your artistry and once you begin to take back your power and take control of your own artistry—especially as a Black Woman—you are now seen as problematic. In contrast to my friend who had to see this shift as a developing adult, I am fortunate that I didn't have this experience until the final semesters of my undergraduate career. I have noticed that Imposter Syndrome has been more prevalent in Black creatives lately and I wish they can realize their worth and truly believe their own hype. As Black people in the arts, we consistently deliver excellence in every artistic medium, but the majority of us somehow feel like we aren't enough, or that our work isn't worthy of praise.

As Black People, Black Professionals, Black Creatives, etc. it's time to believe our own hype because if we don't, nobody else will.

Worth

Nassar Edwards

If there's anything I have ever learned from this past school year it is that "I am worthy."

To be honest, I am still working on it. I actually had to sit myself down and appreciate my accomplishments. I have been going to therapy for the last month and when I began my music education profession, I started to realize my low confidence level. My low confidence and feelings of unworthiness were results of constantly having the fear of failing perfectionism and the feelings of always being behind in my musical journey. My brain always went to the worst possible outcome in any event I did, which I honestly thought was funny until I learned it was unhealthy.

Why did I feel this way?

The school year of 2020-2 1 was in my second school year teaching and will probably be the hardest school year I ever teach. Well that's what every retired and experienced teacher is saying. "It should be a breeze after this."

Will it? Or will the rigor for teachers keep increasing. You have to use more technology, create a bit moji for your

Google classroom, be your children's mentor/counselor/parent/caretaker. These were things I was seeing during the summer of 2020, and honestly I felt a little overwhelmed, especially with my special circumstance.

My first year of teaching, I was an assistant orchestra director with a wonderful co-teacher/mentor. Before my second year of teaching, my co-teacher resigned due to the pandemic. Most teachers were concerned and scared for their families due to the ongoing pandemic. There was also this new trend of teaching in a pandemic called hybrid teaching. If there are words I never want to hear again, it is hybrid teaching.

Hybrid teaching is the art of teaching students in the classroom while also teaching students on Zoom or through some kind of virtual meeting format. States, school districts, and school boards made thousands of teachers risk their lives and mental health to try to make the 2020-21 school year a normal school year. Some people were not about that life and my co-teacher was one of them. I don't blame her and honestly if I didn't have bills to pay I would've resigned too. That put me in an interesting position. I had to act as the head director of an orchestra in the craziest year.

I was honestly scared, but maybe this was *supposed* to happen.

And honestly, a year ago I was looking to be an orchestra teacher anywhere, and it only happened that I ended up teaching with someone. Having another teacher in the classroom with you on a daily basis is so much easier than doing it by yourself. Everyone always thinks the teaching gig is an easy one and anyone can do it, but honestly people don't realize how hard it is until you are actually in the classroom responsible for teaching little human beings whatever material.

But I had to do it, for the kids and myself. So I interviewed for the head director position and was then told my superior/principal I had to prove myself to him that I could do the job. He didn't give me the job, because honestly I only had one year of experience. Another one of my superiors at my school who was in the interview told me she could not see such a young person in such a large position. This honestly crushed my heart, because I thought I was a good enough teacher and the only thing overlooking my dedication and talent was my age. I took the criticism and talked to mentors and my mom and they basically told me I had to prove to those people wrong.

And of course I heard the saying "You know we have to work and be twice as better than white people to get half of what they have" from many other BLACK folks. So I did that. I did not want to think I didn't get the position because I was BLACK, but I would be lying if I said I did not think of it once or twice. I did see many young white head directors receive head director positions straight out of college, but also my principal was another person of color.

So during the pandemic school year I did four concerts, had 55+ kids do solo and ensemble, hosted virtual and safe in-person socials, began livestreaming our concerts, fundraised for our booster club, maintained our social media presence, invited clinicians to work with my kids, taught AP music theory and received all superior ratings for the three ensembles I took to contest.

Was that enough, well I honestly do not know as I am typing this sentence out. I still have not had my second interview with my principal for this head director position and I honestly do not know if I ever will. My principal did say he was proud of my work this school year, but wanted the district to post the job just one more time to see if they are making sure every possible candidate saw this job was available. As I have noticed in the school district I teach in, head director positions, especially high school positions, are usually given to people with multiple years of experience. My position was at the high school level. My principal stated high school teaching positions usually have a higher pool of applicants. After a year of teaching in a global pandemic, that was not the case. There was a national teacher shortage that has caused more stress on school districts, principals and other teachers.

I understand hiring teachers who have a certain amount of experience for certain positions, but I made this job my priority and life during the roughest school year, only just for my confidence and self-worth to be shot down. When our contest results came out, I did not believe or think I deserved the results even though the judges wrote the score and signed their name.

"It wasn't perfect!" I kept saying.

I was expecting perfection from my kids and myself in a pandemic year! For what and who? Oh yes, my principal and for anyone who had an inch of doubt in me. Their doubt translated to me doubting myself. My fear of failing was a constant thought. I could do a task correctly and still have my thoughts telling me I did it wrong or something bad was going to happen. The worst possible outcome always comes to thought. I was surrounded by white colleagues in my profession who had a sheer amount of self-confidence, even if they were wrong. Why couldn't I be like them?

Well because they were always taught to have that confidence. Even if they felt behind, they knew they had the access to catch-up and still succeed while doing the bare minimum. BLACK people in any profession, but especially in music are always told we have to be twice as good to get half of what white people have- you have to struggle to succeed, there's no room to be emotional or depressed.

Well, I am tired of those ideas. Why do I have to mentally and physically abuse myself to prove I can do my job correctly and efficiently? My self is a priority and no job or person or idea should get in the way of it.

The Overlap

A Conversation With Dr. Arris Golden

Lorin: How did you begin your career in music and what makes you continue to want to pursue a career in this field?

Arris: I feel like I started in the same way that most musicians do. I started piano lessons in second grade, I started beginning band in sixth grade...nothing terribly exciting. I think that the difference for me, the thing that brought me to where I am currently, is what happened once I arrived at UNC-Chapel Hill...and also the second time I attended UNC (another story for another day…).

I think that we as musicians tend to have a "difference maker:" Someone or several someones that inspire us to become performers or educators. For me, this happened my junior year of college, though I did not realize it at the time. At the end of sophomore year, the director of bands retired and after a search, the university hired his replacement. As a part of the student membership on that committee, I had *no idea* that, upon arrival my junior year, the person that was hired (who was our choice collectively):

1.) Had a spouse that would join him on the music education faculty and become an incredible

> influence on my life as a musician and educator;
>
> 2.) Would ask all of us to work harder and demand more from ourselves than we thought possible; I should add that we *hated* him for making changes and insisting that we adjust our lived experiences to move forward; and finally
>
> 3.) Inspire us to achieve our goals through that process in ways that still resonate with me today. It is that experience, that inspiration from someone who thought that anything was possible if you "did your work" that brought me to where I am today and that keeps me moving forward through this profession.

Lorin: Intersectionality is defined as an analytical framework for understanding how aspects of a person's social and political identities combine to create different modes of discrimination and privilege. With you being not only a woman but a Black woman within a white, male dominated industry, have you felt the effects of intersectionality?

Arris: Easy answer: Yes, of course. More difficult answer: Yes, of course, and I have yet to figure out how to separate the two. *How does one determine if one is being left out or held back in a space because of those particular intersections.* And I say this, because they really do feel much the same, with little variance from situation to situation. And I would also add that these same exact qualities actually have opened doors for me in this profession. They have secured honor bands for me; they have secured employment as an adjudicator for me; they have also supported me in employment throughout my time as both a collegiate and public school educator. It is, to me, truly a double-edged sword, with a positive and negative side. And perhaps, it is "separateable" by comparing the experiences of my women colleagues in this field, but I am not certain that approaching it in that way would reveal the differences that this question alludes to.

Lorin: On my podcast, *Relative Pitch*[1], we talked about the ways in which we feel as if we as minorities and POC have to work much harder to get to the same places and positions that our white colleagues get to. This brought on a conversation about impostor syndrome and belonging. What advice can you give to anyone experiencing the effects of impostor syndrome? How do you deal with it?

Arris: Ideal with this in two ways. First, and luckily, I have a best friend who REFUSES to let me undersell myself. Like, REFUSES. And she gets very "in my face" about it when she hears me not take a compliment or not acknowledge an achievement. And I am very thankful that she does that.

Second, I have reached a point in my existence that I am just very in tune (pun intended, I guess) with what I am capable of doing. I have worked *hard* to learn all the things I have learned and to be able to do the things that I do and I know that I do them well. As that same best friend of mine would say, "You have to own your own greatness." No one else is going to do that for you and when that "voice in your head" starts with all the doubt that inevitably comes around, you have to be stubborn with yourself in reminding yourself that you are *capable*. You have done the work and you have every right to occupy the space that you are present in.

Lorin: Do you feel like you have a responsibility as a female conductor of color to program and uplift music by other minority and POC composers? What is your process for choosing repertoire?

Arris: Yes, I do. And I would also add women composers to that list. I also think that it is just as big a responsibility to program the music of minority, POC, and women composers in ways that spotlight their place in the canon of band music. What does that mean? It means that my ultimate goal is to program works by these composers throughout the academic year, preferably within each concert cycle, in ways that allow the listener and the performers to see and understand that their music belongs within the established wind band canon. That it has a place beside Grainger, Hindemith, Reed,Holst,Vaughan Williams, and all the other white composers that we have deemed "standard." Their music should not be tokenized or singled out for "one-off programs" (think "____________________ Month program"). Their music can and *should be* programmed in the same way that we would program any other music for our ensembles.

Lorin: How does it make you feel to see musicians of color within our field? What more do you think can be done in terms of diversity, inclusion, and equity within our field?

Arris: Both excited and invigorated at the possibilities of what will come. But I think that to continue this process, to really achieve the diverse, inclusive, and equitable settings

that we all envision, we have to start earlier than most places and spaces realize. One really great example of this is the Crescendo Detroit Program, created by Damien Crutcher (https://www.crescendodetroit.org/the-purpose/).
This program establishes connections to the arts for students of color earlier than our current norm and gets them excited and involved in the arts. Their purpose statement says it all:

> *Our* MISSION *is to transform the lives of youth, ages 5-18, in the neighborhoods in which we operate by developing intense instrumental music, vocal music and dance programs that promote artistic excellence and character building. Using a youth-centered approach we will offer a comprehensive program that also includes literacy and lifeskills classes, homework support, and daily meals and snacks. Our* VISION *is to create and develop arts-centered neighborhood programs in the city of Detroit that build character in youth and foster a love for and participation in the arts.*

Lorin: What's a song you listen to when you feel like you need to reconnect with music?

Arris: *JUST ONE?* That's not going to work for me...but I will try to not go overboard...I'll do a "top five-ish" instead:

1. Sweet Love—Anita Baker

2. Barely Breathing—Duncan Sheik

3. As—Stevie Wonder

4. Mathisder Mahler—Paul Hindemith (SFO with Blomstedt version only, please)

5. Drivin'—Everything But the Girl

6. Golden—Jill Scott

7. Trouble—Ray LaMontagne

Each of these songs will make me stop what I am doing and just listen to the music. Additionally, each of these songs has the ability to pull me out of a bad mood/bad headspace/bad thought process and recenter my state of being. I think it is because of the construction of each song, coupled with the text and perhaps also the connections that these songs bring to mind: life experiences, performances, and people.

Breaking Point

Nicholas A. Felder

I have been asking myself these questions of who I am

As a person,

As an individual

As an artist.

And asking,

"What does it mean… to become… me?

And what does it mean to become… '**BLACK**'?

Because I've been BLACK my entire life…"

Thinking myself an imposter in my own skin.

Tear-
ing myself across____
the rigid And the
beautiful—

The harsh *diss*onance from my body
And the spiritual lyricism…

…in my soul.

But I have decided *not* to
limit myself—To be part
of one thing
And everything at the same time.

Because I am me,

I am ME

And I will *not*

allow myself

to retreat

Or SHRINK inside.

Because I have *hit* my breaking point—

No return.

2 The reason I choose not to capitalize "white" is because I am speaking on a more abstract level—"white" as an environment that amplifies divergence, to the point of ostracization—in addition to referring to the historical background of the race.

Author's Note:
This poem was originally written in response to a piece I wrote for violin, bassoon and piano. The poem experiments with the concept that Blackness takes up space and appears as a spectacle against a white background. It also illustrates my personal relationship with Blackness—something I was born with but also alienated from as my self-perception traveled away from the particular aesthetic imposed on me through the media and my peers.

Consequently, many of my thoughts and emotions were repressed and denied for a long time, attempting to squish them into nonexistence. Allowing myself to finally confront these suppressed emotions and experiences—speaking my mind unapologetically—was painful yet also deeply liberating.

The Divide

Nicholas A. Felder

What has it been like for me, as a person of color, in the classical music world? Probably quite similar to a lot of people's experiences, to be honest. I'd like to say I was more aware of the lack of diversity in orchestra classes and rehearsals (I mean, I noticed there were a lot more Asian and White kids than Black kids), but I think I just accepted it—or at least thought of it as a norm that wasn't going to change anytime soon.

The thing is, I've been immersed in "classical music" since my years in cherub choir at an Episcopal church (another White-dominant environment), so I was more acclimated with that culture when I started playing violin in the fifth grade. I only learned more about playing other music styles like pop, jazz, and r&b when I moved to Atlanta, Georgia and took lessons from someone who specialized in them. For the first time, I realized what it meant to open up and not obsess over the exact notes on a page—to listen to the harmonies and rhythms and create my own space in the music. I suppose you could say this was also the first time I started to compose music.

Of course, unfortunately, that side of myself went dormant again when I decided I wanted to pursue music as a career—that is, classical music. Why was there this "divide"? Why did

I think I had a potentially prosperous future playing with an orchestra in a concert hall and not as a violinist in a band? It seemed like these binaries had been infused in my brain since elementary school—particularly when my family moved to a more affluent (Whiter) part of town in Spring, Texas.

There was then the side of me that loved singing out and dancing to Diana Ross, Cheryl Lynn and Stevie Wonder (although if you had asked me their names at the time, I, being a clueless 9-year old, would've given a blank look) and the side of me that was quiet and shy and "colored inside the lines." While I don't think I ever code-switched, I do think I experienced a dramatic shift in my perception of the world—transitioning from a minority-dominant neighborhood where everyone knew everyone on the street, and the barbershop, just at the front of the neighborhood, was a whole community in itself to a white-dominant neighborhood where all the houses were huge, everyone had the latest gadgets, and groups just seemed a bit more exclusive.

I relate all of this from my childhood because I think that was the first ingraining of some sort of binary—a divide and disparity—between White people and people of color (POC). What started out as a move evolved and seeped into my perceptions of music—"classical" vs. "pop". The obvious issue here is that the two are not mutually exclusive. Music can be classical (characteristic of a culture's roots) as well as popular (there was a time when "classical music" was just popular music).

I continue to ponder this now, not only with my own life and how to reform my own views, but also how to use my experiences and what I've learned to give the next generation of musicians and artists the "culturally sustaining" space that I did not have. I want to help debunk this "individualist" mentality and raise up community-centered work. To create a place where everyone's views, values, cultures and identities are realized, respected and celebrated. A place where we all come together to do the work.

It is this community around which an ideal world, without the "divide", can manifest. Because that's how Black artists, and Black people as a whole, escaped—how they transcended—their entrapment. However, it is not only about the artists embracing this collective bond but also about the world fully welcoming it and all the identities involved. The ideal world is a place without dissonance between the creation and reception of a kind of music (as the first note breaks the atmosphere). Where every crack and lilt are heard for what they are.

What if we just listened to someone as if hearing music for the first time? Something that is so tethered to history and what we think we know yet also inherently new? If music can be described as the breath of humans, then it, too, will and must be allowed to evolve and shift and diverge and converge in a glorious enigma of ways. Music is about purely acting on instinct—what it truly means to be human—and if we are to survive, it is a freedom we need to embrace.

There aren't any moments in my musical background that stick out to me as a time when I was discriminated against as a musician of color, but I do think all my experiences together had a significant influence and impact on my view of music and the world. The moment I was taught the "divide" and how I could be or express myself one way but not another—that was the problem. It was like I was only free to voice one side of myself—the side that was "accepted" in the classical music world.

Because I didn't know any better, and I was naturally

a kid who liked "neatness" and "coloring inside the lines," I submitted to all the rules and "hegemonic, essentialist thinking." Just imagine if I had been exposed to more ways of thinking—more perspectives of history, math, science, literature and music earlier in life, in the classroom, and rehearsals as well as with my family and friends.

Masking Everything: #BlackInTheArts

Sydnee Goode

I was doing so well until everything changed.

Before the pandemic, I was growing as a musician and an individual. I finally felt sure of myself and I became more confident in my talents and my choices. However, March 13, 2020 has changed my life for… better or for worse, am I right?

Friday, March 13, 2020 was the day the students at my university were told to move out of the dorms and quarantine because of the spread of the virus. My choir peers and I were on a bus back from Alabama when we found out the world officially stopped. People were infected, hospitalized, and dying without getting the chance to see their loved ones. 2020 was dreadful and probably the worst year of most people's lives. Some positive things happened while we were in quarantine, but more negative things happened.

While in quarantine, all citizens were advised to wear a mask in public. At the time, it was fine, but now I feel like I am losing myself. After wearing a mask for over a year and a half, I can't seem to find any stability or understanding. Not only have I lost the chance to have a normal college experience, but I feel as though I have lost the chance to grow as a musical individual. Everyone wears a mask as a shield to protect themselves and others from the virus, but who is to say that the mask isn't shielding other things? What if some people use the mask as a shield to hide from others? What if "some people" just so happens to be me?

Since wearing the mask, the confidence that I grew pre-quarantine has gone. For some time, I have come to terms with the fact that I am using this mask as an aid to hide my true self from the rest of this world. Not only has this taken a physical toll on me, but it has also taken a mental toll on me. I am not an expressive person and I do not like attention being drawn on me; the mask worsened everything. Now, I use it like a safety blanket.

Wearing a mask means that I don't have to face reality. No one questions my behavior and no one questions the various faces I make. No one tells me to "smile more" and no one asks me how I am. I don't have to be what people expect me to be. Why is it that the society we live in teaches us to act like anything and anybody but ourselves?

In May of 2020, the world changed. As a Black woman living in "the land of the free", I felt trapped. My Black peers and I had to watch our brothers and sisters get brutalized and harmed by the very people who swore to protect us. Black lives mattered… or so I thought. In addition to that, the School of Music within my university did absolutely nothing to reassure their Black students.

The professors who I once believed I could confide in let my peers and I grieve with no reassurance or empathy. With that in mind, a few of my Black colleagues and I came together to bring light and hope to this dark situation. We created a group called the Black Musicians Coalition; this group was created for Black musicians for Black musicians. After producing our show The Blueprint: **#BlackInTheArts** in Spring 2021 and garnering support from our community, there was a question that lingered in our heads: How is it that the very students who "make" the program are the same ones who are left behind?

That's it. That's your answer. Being **#BlackInTheArts** is being left behind and never thought of until needed. We are the forces within these programs that help it succeed and our innovations and creativity make the world go round. Without us, there would be nothing.

Being **#BlackInTheArts** is having auditions for your school's production of The Wiz and a white girl asking if she has to "talk uneducated" for her audition. Being #BlackInTheArts is watching the production of The Wiz fall apart and be executed poorly because your white peers do not want to work as hard for a Black-centered musical. Being #BlackInTheArts is having your peers automatically assume you have a soulful voice. Being #BlackInTheArts is auditioning for roles knowing that you probably won't get any because you don't "fit the part." Being #BlackInTheArts is having to work twice as hard for opportunities to only get half of what your white peers have. Being #BlackInTheArts is having older white people confuse you with the other Black woman in your choir. Being #BlackInTheArts is beautiful until it's not.

Black students deserve better. We want the same opportunities as our white peers, but we must work harder and show less of ourselves to be deemed as acceptable and compliant. With that being said, it is time for me to take a stand and be the person I wish my younger self could look up to. Like a wall, the mask that I once wore to hide myself is slowly falling.

Flute & Fate: Finding My Way

A Conversation with Ashley Crawford

Choosing Music

Lorin: What was your experience with choosing to study music?

Ashley: I initially wanted to be a band director. Seeing the passion of my band directors when they would teach and conduct was inspirational. I always felt the fire from that and wanted to be in that space, so I started to learn. It began with learning conducting patterns, standing on a podium running sectionals, or being in different leadership positions that would allow me to feel a bit of that energy of being in front of musicians. By the time I went off to college, I had decided to major in music education. After taking a few ed classes in my sophomore year, I reached a point in Applied Lessons that piqued my interest more than secondary education. My flute instructor, Ms. Belinda Laupp, helped me realize I could bring something different to flute performance and explore various opportunities within the field of music. I switched to liberal arts and focused solely on my performance career. I no longer envisioned myself in the K-12 classroom setting. In grad school, I majored in flute pedagogy and classical music performance. I found my own lane and, to this day, continue to curate spaces for myself to exist in. As far as pedagogy is concerned, that's where my skills as a flute professor and choir conductor shine.

Lorin: I can't imagine the impact you have on your students, being who you are in general. Can you speak on that?

Ashley: When I arrived at TSU in 2016, my online persona at that time centered around makeup and natural hair. So, when I first got there and started to recruit for my studio, they thought I was pretty cool.

Many of them had no idea I was a flutist. However, we immediately hit it off because my social media content at the time created relatability between us. The following spring semester, the #MaskOffChallenge happened, and it changed everything. The students were traveling with the band then, so it took them by surprise to see one of their professors go viral for playing classical flute on a Hip-Hop song. This moment positively impacted my studio because I could reach my students moving forward entirely. This was also the moment "FluteBae," was birthed. To see a young, black female professor live authentically inspired them in more ways than one.

Teaching and Pedagogy

Lorin: How did you first get into your teaching position and how you have managed being in it?

Ashley: After finishing my master's degree in 2014,

I immediately went on the audition circuit for major symphonies. Things didn't go my way. So, then I faced the dilemma, what will I do now? Some college jobs opened up, and I applied for them. In doing so, I contacted professors from my Master's program for letters of recommendation. I was met with reluctance due to the school being "heavily researched based." Facing this type of response felt very backhanded and microaggressive. Around this time, my undergrad teacher retired and recommended I take her place. Unfortunately, they decided to go with someone else despite high recommendations from several people. Moving forward, I decided to teach privately until something else came along. I reached out to band directors from underserved schools and began teaching students who had never experienced private lessons. I did this for a year until TSU called again, needing a flute instructor. The person they hired didn't work out. I happily took over in Fall 2016. Tennessee State University's Flute Studio has been flourishing ever since. This transition was an interesting time for me, especially being a musician and creative. I had to learn entrepreneurial skills because there wasn't a guarantee I'd be hired anywhere. Although I'd achieved many accolades and degrees, I was still made to feel like I wasn't good enough. I had to create opportunities for myself to succeed in this field. A mentor of mine once told me this will be the most political place you will ever work in higher academia. And that has been true for the last six years I've been there. I managed it by staying authentic to myself and who I am as a flutist.

Non-Traditional Teaching

Lorin: Your teaching style is very well-rounded and inclusive of methods that are not often seen in western classical spaces. Can you speak on your pedagogical viewpoint?

Ashley: Many educators hold on to this antiquated way of teaching. They often try to deem what is considered a real success in music. I even had to check myself in my teaching style because I'm so trained that I thought everybody was supposed to be taught the same way. Everybody has to stick to one curriculum, and that's not the case. For example, I have flutists who just want to improv and learn jazz or hip hop. In taking on the online persona, "FluteBae," I opened myself up to many different types of flutists. I had to break out of that box quickly. If I'm going to play this way, I have to be able to teach this way too. Yes, classical training is necessary for some spaces, but not all. Some flutists express themselves differently, and embracing that is okay. There are so many living composers and genres to explore. We don't have to subscribe to just one westernized academic way of thinking. Music and creativity are about expanding and pushing the envelope. That is what made the performers and composers before us legendary.

NAAWS

Lorin: Can you talk about the Nashville African American Wind Symphony's (NAAWS) creation and your Juneteenth debut concert?

Ashley: On June 19th, 2022, NAAWS performed their debut in McAfee Hall at Belmont University in Nashville, Tn. We worked for months to make it to our debut. This moment was full circle for me. When I was a student at Belmont, I sometimes was the only black person in the symphony or on stage. On this day, an all-black ensemble performed a repertoire of works by black composers, and it was such a powerful moment. I'm grateful the community got to experience this moment and can't wait to share what else is in store for NAAWS, Inc.

Reference Recordings

Lorin: Are there going to be reference recordings from your Juneteenth performance?

Ashley: Yes, recordings can be found at www.naawsmusic.org.

Going Forward

Lorin: What do you want to see in the next year, 5 years, and 10 years within classical music? How do we make this field actually equitable? How do we make sure that the next generation of young black students who want to go into music don't have to face as many things that you or even I have had to endure? What does that look like?

It starts with leadership. It begins with people not being afraid to have these conversations and dance around the issues. The possibility of white fragility or somebody getting their feelings hurt because the topic of discussion is race should not sway leadership from having hard conversations. Many think racism is simply calling someone the "N-word" and not liking someone because they're black. No, it goes way deeper than that. It is a complete system, and this system has infiltrated our institutions all over the country. We need fearless leaders who aren't afraid to diversify. Diversify the symphonies and music faculties. There are black musicians all over this country. It doesn't make sense not to have more representation of us. We need leaders who are not afraid to have the conversation but are also not scared of the backlash. You have to be ready to fight against the rebuttal. When people try to back you against the wall, slap a muzzle on you, and say, "Hey, we don't want to talk about race because it makes us uncomfortable." Leadership needs to stand up and say, "Let's get uncomfortable together," because the issue won't get fixed unless it is addressed. Systemic racism won't disappear because it isn't discussed. Realize that we are human and are created equal.

Ashley: My degree isn't any less than yours, and my intellect isn't any less than yours. These institutions claim to be equal-opportunity employers. Well, prove it. It starts from the top. There are black students majoring in various music concentrations, and they deserve the same opportunities as their white/non-black counterparts. Unwavering and progressive leadership can make this happen.

Time Will Tell:
The Innate Toxicity of Classical Music Culture from the Perspective of a Black Woman Violinist

Camille Jones

Introduction

There is a pervasive sense of toxicity within the classical music community that many people are aware of and just okay with. It's important to note that the problems that classical musicians face are by no means unique to our community. These are issues that are reflective of society as a whole. However, in order to break down macro-level issues, we have to work to eliminate the problem in smaller increments (i.e. within our individual communities). Although I am just one person and therefore can only provide insight into these problems through my own perspective, I hope that my personal experiences will touch people. I hope that in the end, some will feel seen by my story, and others will read it and contemplate the institutions that they uphold. Below, I will discuss my thoughts regarding various issues facing music academia and the importance of mental health for BIPOC in a predominantly white field.

Music Academia

One of the biggest flaws in music academia is the lack of care towards each students' varied upbringings. There is a lack of understanding of the privileges that any student entering college may or may not have in regards to the kind of music education they've received prior. When I entered college, I did not carry the sort of familiarity that many of my white peers seemed to have about studying classical music. I didn't come from a family of musicians and I couldn't afford the best private instruction, therefore I had to figure out a lot of things on my own. I took one music theory class (the only one offered at my public high school) before entering college. I also started a little late compared to most students I knew in college (9 or 10), so you could say I was at a little bit of a disadvantage because of that as well. Most of my knowledge around classical music came from outside of public school at a youth orchestra (located in a predominantly white county of Maryland) or attending mini summer programs. It's interesting because I think a lot of why I have a complicated relationship with classical music now stems from my early years studying the genre in middle school and high school. A time period where I was a little naive or still coming to terms with my own identity as a young Black girl studying the violin. I say all of this not to garner some sort of pity, but to provide context so that you may understand the full picture.

When I began my freshman year of college, I experienced culture shock. Even though I had been surrounded by white peers at that aforementioned youth orchestra, I came from the very diverse county of Prince George's, Maryland. I had the privilege of growing up with a lot of kids who looked like me and whenever I did go to those youth orchestra rehearsals a couple times a week I had experienced what I would later realize to be culture shocks on a smaller scale. However, when I went to college at a PWI (predominantly white institution), I experienced a culture shock on a much larger scale. I had also entered while Trump was running for president. I will talk more about the psychological implications of all of this later, but needless to say, I had a difficult time acclimating to my new environment. There were plenty of times where I had imposter syndrome[1] and felt like I just didn't belong. It was like I went into college and many of my white classmates seemed to have so much more musical experience than I had, or at least they presented themselves that way·Those feelings were only amplified anytime a white professor decided to make an insensitive comment towards me or about a subject that affected me. The following anecdotes do not serve to call out anyone, but to bring awareness to the types of experiences Black music students may have in college and to inspire change.

I remember one particular instance during my sophomore year where I was struggling with music theory. I tried articulating my confusion, but I was met with an attitude/tone which said, "there's nothing wrong with my teaching style so what's wrong with you?" to which I actually replied, "well I guess I'm just stupid" sarcastically. To my dismay, the professor actually nodded as if to say "yeah maybe" but couldn't bring himself to fully verbalize the words. In another instance, one professor repeatedly asked me condescending

[1]Ebony McGee, "Impostor Syndrome? No. Just Racism." University World News, 5 June 2021; see also Ruchika Tulshyan and Jodi-Ann Burey, "Stop Telling Women They Have Imposter Syndrome." Harvard Business Review, 31 Mar. 202. The use of the term imposter syndrome can be seen as controversial as it tends to disregard systemic issues related to feelings of self-worth. These two articles delve deeper into these issues and the widely accepted psychological definition of imposter syndrome.

questions like, "do you know your right from your left?" when I didn't understand a particular instruction. They also indirectly said I was not a fun student to work with because I had certain skills that needed improvement. Almost more disappointing than the insults of professors were the insensitive remarks of some of my colleagues. I remember being paired with a particular pianist (before I knew that she was also Black) and asked my colleagues about her casually because I hadn't heard of her before. The first thing one girl said was "I don't know her well, but I know she isn't White or Asian", as if that was the only thing of importance to know about her. All of these examples of microaggression really boiled over to become something that largely impacted how I viewed music academia and those that uphold it as a whole.

While I dealt with these struggles on a daily basis, I had to also come to terms with not only the visual underrepresentation of people who looked like me at my school, but also the extreme reverence for old white men in the music we studied. The longer I studied as an undergrad, the more I began to struggle with the idea of performing and supporting works by composers like Mozart, Schubert, or Beethoven (save the debate for later, Beethoven read as white to his colleagues)[2]. I eventually felt the need to take

2 The Beethoven is Black debate has been around for decades, recently resurfacing last year during the coronavirus pandemic. It is hotly debated due to the idea that someone who is highly revered among white scholars (and classical musicians generally) as a musical genius – a title not often awarded to Black people – could be of African descent. Regardless of whether Beethoven had any African heritage, he was largely treated as a white composer in a white supremacist society. Read more about this debate from German history professor and musicologist Dr. Kira Thurman: @kirathurman (Kira Thurman) "Hi gang! I'm not on twitter much right now, but because several of you have asked for my take on the question, 'Was Beethoven Black?'..." Twitter, 18 June 2020. https://twitter.com/kira_thurman/status/1273664572453539843

matters into my own hands (as I've come to find many young BIPOC do) and create my own concert series titled Voices Unheard[3] that was specifically centered around BIPOC voices. This series was a turning point for me because it became my one opportunity at my school to really indulge in music by BIPOC composers and also share this music with my colleagues. Although I felt that the enthusiasm/ support surrounding these concerts could have been better, I am thankful that the school provided the opportunity by hosting these concerts on campus. While I am grateful for this little victory, it doesn't negate the fact that I largely felt I had to prove myself more than my whiter counterparts for the majority of my undergraduate years.

Mental Health

What I would truly like for white professors and music directors to understand is just how much weight their actions and words hold on different people. The side effect of being ignorant to diverse voices in music education for the majority of their careers is that they silently tell their students of color over and over that they don't really belong. The kicker is that not only have they refused to broaden their perspectives for the majority of their careers, but many PWI's and conservatories don't even have a safe outlet for BIPOC music students to properly voice their frustrations. The ending result being a lot of pent-up frustration with nowhere to go without the right resources and support system. Of course, things are starting to look a little brighter in the classical music realm these days due to the global racial reckoning that erupted in 2020. However, let's really consider

3 https://voicesunheardproject.org/

what it cost: the murder of another Black man at the hands of police (and during a pandemic no less). On a similar note, I really want to stress again how much mental wellness matters, especially within the Black community. While I was attending college, I was under a lot of mental stress. Not only due to the regular school pressures and microaggressions, but because of what was happening in the world. The murder of an unarmed Black man would be on the news and I would go to school and pretend like I didn't want to explode inside. I remember when I saw Stephon Clark (a 22-year-old shot and killed in his grandmother's backyard) on the news and wanted so badly to direct my anger at my colleagues for not even pretending to care, probably because they just didn't even notice. There were also other racially motivated crimes that happened on campus, and still I felt close to nothing from my white and non-Black peers. But maybe it's my fault for wanting something from them that they just weren't capable of giving at the time.

Another interesting trope I would like to discuss which is often seen in the classical music realm is that of a toxic student/teacher relationship. You know, the one that values tough love, especially that coming from an older white man. The one where studio professors cross certain boundaries with their words (and sometimes their actions) because they feel they can and because they think it's "good for you," just character development. It's that sort of relationship that hides sexism beneath a glamour. I find it so bizarre actually that there are many people who know of professors who are very "particular" to say the least about who joins their studio. Furthermore, when you throw race into the question of this tired dynamic, things really start to take a turn for the worse. The last thing I will say about this is that we need to critically analyze the white men in music professions and stop OK'ing those who are known to be arrogant, disrespectful, and discriminatory.

Conclusion

I challenge arts administrators at predominantly white schools and other white and non-Black classical musicians to take a step back and truly analyze their practices. Make a conscious effort to uplift Black student voices by challenging traditional music curriculums and by having open ears. It's very easy to say you value the voices of others and support them, but without following through with tangible actions, those words fall short. Accept criticism and recognize that it's okay to make mistakes, but be willing to learn and grow from them, never settle. I would also advise white administrators and musicians to take a pause before starting new diversity initiatives under their name if there was no initial effort made to support existing BIPOC-led initiatives and organizations. Finally, I would just like to say that while I've struggled to keep my faith in the classical music genre over the past few years, I have genuinely been impressed by the amazing organizations and initiatives that my colleagues of color have jump started and been a part of. I am proud to know and work with these individuals and I do have hope for the future of classical music to be even more than it is now. As with all things, however, time will tell.

Trust in You!

Anthony Morris

"Trust your gift because there is no one in the world who can do what God wants YOU to do" — Niecy Nash

The first questions that pop into my head when I walk into a room, specifically a room full of musicians, are:

> *"Do I belong here?",*
>
> *"Why am I the only one that looks like me?"*
>
> *"Am I here for someone else's agenda?"*

The power of imposter syndrome has always been the little devil on my shoulder since beginning music but it became very apparent during my collegiate career. During this time, I began to really question my skills and always asking myself "Am I as good as my counterparts?" It felt like no matter how hard I tried or actually achieved, I was always second best. Of course, that led me down a wrenching spiral of always second-guessing myself. Music always came naturally to me, no matter if it was making my parents take me to piano lessons at 10 o'clock in the morning every Saturday, singing with my Baptist church choir, or even playing at regional conferences.

Even though I became "successful" in music, I never truly felt like I fit in. I remember being at All-State conferences and never finding people who were like me. My first All-State conference was one of the first times where I was completely aware of my Blackness in the musical arts. As I looked out into the choir, I did not see a lot of Black musicians. Because there were very few of us, we mostly stayed silent during breaks while our other colleagues sang every musical theatre song they could imagine. They felt comfortable, we did not. After my first experience at All-State, I went back to my school and started thinking of music differently. I started to see it differently.

I continued my path through music which ended up leading to some great accomplishments for myself. I ended up doing All-State for the rest of my years at high school, performing with my band and choir at conferences, and even became the drum major of my high school marching band. Becoming a drum major was one of the most defining moments of my life. I had to fight for that spot. I auditioned two years in a row. I didn't get it my first year and that really sparked a fire in me because I had worked so hard for it but didn't get it for reasons unknown to me. Of course, my imposter syndrome kicked in gear and I had many different conspiracies of why I didn't get it.

Sometime later, I actually found out it was true. I took all the negativities of this experience and started to hone in on my craft of conducting. I wanted to be the best so that no one could even think of saying no.

Conducting has become naturally my passion. I have

fallen in love with the art of conducting and each day it festers more. I have started to participate in symposiums throughout the past year and one thing I have noticed from all of them is that there is a lack of and absence of people who look like me. I later thought to myself,

"Who are the Black wind band conductors that are not at an HBCU?"

I could not come up with that many. I believe that needs to change for the next generation of young Black boys and girls who find music and conducting interesting. I want them to say, "oh, I believe I can do that," instead of second-guessing if they should be in this field like I have. We need to be more diverse in both conducting and music. We need more Black men and women wind band conductors to influence the current state and upcoming state of music. I am glad for opportunities like the Mike Moss Study Grant which is allowing minorities to experience the art of conducting and developing their love for music. I would like to bridge the way into opening conversations and providing a change to the current demographics of a field that I love. I am tired of second-guessing if I am in the right field, I know that I am meant to be here.

As I have grown in the music field, I have realized that I needed to surround myself with positive influences which include lifelong mentors and friends who will continue to lift me up. This field can seem very lonely at times, especially being a person of color. I remember hearing the phrase "It takes a whole village to raise a child" and I have developed my village that will help me on my journey to become the best musician I can be. Although my village is strong and will always have my back, I have also realized that I must take action for myself. I always remind myself that I can take no one else's path but my own for my future. I have to trust in myself because there is no one in the world who can do what God wants me to do.

The Caucasity; The Litany; The Truth

Wendy Caudle Hodge

While Standing in line to get student IDs

Me: "What do you play?"

White dude: "Trumpet. What about you?"

Me: "I play the oboe."

White dude: "You're not an oboe player. Oboe players are...... (long awkward pause). geeks."

Me: "um....Thanks?"

While mingling with big donors at a Symphony fundraiser, greeting them and thanking them for their support...

Me (greeting a small group of old white people): Good evening, thank you for supporting the arts. Are you enjoying the party?

Old white lady: Yes, we love coming to the symphony. Did you help organize the event this year?

Me: No Ma'am, I play in the symphony.

Old white lady: Really? I don't remember seeing YOU on stage. Hon, you're so pretty I thought you were one of the basketball player's wives.

Me: !!!...???......uhhh....thank you????

Backstage conversation with a "colleague"

Me: Do you have a plaque I can borrow?

White girl (Freelancer playing the concert): Yeah, grab one from the tin on top of my case. Just don't steal anything.

Me: !!!. You know what, I'm good.

20 years...
20 ....years......
2 to the zero years............

- Of enduring isolation in the workplace
- Of thinking/hoping "This is a different Orchestra so it will be a different experience"
- Of feeling uncomfortable about suggesting Black composers
- Of actively trying to be open-minded and give colleagues a chance.. Or second chance
- Of saying to myself "she/he didn't mean it that way"

- Of agonizing over which incidents to let go and which incidents to bring up,
- Of knowing your concerns about your work environment will be dismissed
- Of playing the music of the oppressors
- Of hearing "YOU play the oboe?"
- Of knowing it's because I'm Black
- Of knowing no one would believe me if I pointed out the racism in the work place
- Of listening to white people get excited about the concerts in February because the music we play is so much "fun, interesting or unusual"
- Of searching for oboe literature written by Black composers and none of my teachers could point me to more than 3 works. The oboe has at least a 400 year history.
- Of surprised/quizzical/confused looks when I meet a new student for the first time.
- Of surprised/quizzical/confused looks when I show up for a free-lance gig
- Of justifying my fees
- Of being underestimated
- Of hearing in a surprised voice "Wow, you're really good."
- Of loving the music of the oppressors and feeling guilty about it
- Of knowing I can't trust my colleagues
- Of knowing every performance is a justification of my presence/job
- Of almost never seeing anyone that looks like me at work
- Of code switching at work
- Of worrying about driving home after playing at

venues in the South
- Of still being shocked at the racist things white people do
- Of being over prepared
- Of people assuming I sing gospel, the blues or jazz when they hear I'm a musician
- Of being nervous to wear my hair in braids, locs or natural at work
- Of listening to all white music at the Christmas party
- Of shattering the myth that full lips make playing the oboe more difficult
- Of being expected to speak for all Black people
- Of feeling pressure to represent all Black people in the classical music space
- Of working extremely hard to cultivate professional relationships that came naturally to my peers.
- Of being #BlackInTheArts

The truth is, after being Black the next identifier I would choose is artist/creative.

Even though my profession, my chosen discipline, my creative outlet has been music for such a long time I've realized that I shouldn't limit my creativity. As an artist/creative, I'm very proud to have the ability to bring abstract concepts to life, to give new meaning to old ideas, to insert my perspective and experience into the creative process, to innovate, to transform, to be a change agent.

I've used my talent to transition into a career in government. That means I now have the ability to directly impact lives for the better, to bring beauty into the community I serve, to give hope and help to the most vulnerable, to push for meaningful change in policy and procedure that will improve quality of life and give a voice to the voiceless.

Our voices, perspective and talents must be present in all spaces and even though I'm not making music everyday that doesn't mean I'm not an artist.

I've just switched my outlet.

Am I Invisible?

Jammie Phillips

When I am the only Black woman at your Flute symposium?

When I outplay everyone in the section and seated 3rd chair
since I'm the only one that can't afford to take lessons?

When I'm a consecutively superior rated and; consistent band
director, male band directors only call upon me to work the
Flute section instead of the entire band.

When I attend a conference for women band directors,
I listen to white women who are collegiate directors at
prestigious universities discuss their plight
of being overlooked by men, knowing that men and white
women ignore me.

When I know that there are only certain schools and certain
school districts that would hire me because not only am I

Black, I'm a woman, and there is a Historically Black College and University on my resume.

When in a competition room with colleagues from other school districts,
I get left out of any conversation among the other directors.

When I never made it on the email list for a community orchestra, but was asked to join the second year in the ensemble. Is this done on purpose because I am the only Black woman participating?

I know that I will never be able to afford that **$10,000** flute because my parents struggle to pay the bills.

When I sit next to the white woman or male in the section for the first time, they are pleasantly surprised that I can play. Don't we all learn the same notes and rhythms?

I have to major in Music Education and become a teacher because performance as a career is not feasible for my family.

As a Black woman in music, being in the same position as our counterparts is nearly impossible.

Being a Black woman from the hood, it is impossible.

Making the impossible possible is my presence and my plight to be respected.

You will acknowledge me.

My Life as a Double-Edged Sword

Andrew Wynn

The Illinois Chapter

It would come much of a surprise to many people that I meet that I am a GAY, African American male. My mom was white, and my dad is Black; I was born into this world already detested by many groups of people. I grew up in a meth-addled town in Southern Illinois where white teenagers flew the confederate flag to show off their "indomitable" freedom. To most of us in the POC community of Olney, Illinois, this sole act was out of sheer ignorance and the lack of wanting to understand the gruesome history of the "Stars and Bars." It was not a symbol of "individual freedom of oppression" but more of a symbol of oppression. In my elementary and middle school days, I vividly remember being able to count on my hands the number of Black students within my schools. Even in elementary school, I remember being outcasted for my skin color with my white-washed city. In middle school, I went on a route of self-discovery and came out as gay in the 7th grade. I thought that everyone would be ok with it, but I was so wrong. A city with the religious interest much akin to a agnostic sect has much to say to a gay, Black student. Many times I was told that I should kill myself or I will go to hell all because I preferred the same gender. The "normal" white heterosexual students in my school were not able to understand why I felt the way I did after being singled out for my sexuality and race; it is understandable that it is an alien concept to them, but human decency "should" come into play in these situations. How many of you that are reading this can remember walking through the hallways of your middle school and the other boys in your grade or higher covering their crotch area and asking you, "what are you looking at f**?" Or having the n word thrown at you like it is nothing? I can only partially blame them because those are things that they learned from their parents or older siblings. It can be seen as not only a generational issue, but as an intelligence issue as well.

The Alabama Chapter

After my eighth-grade year of middle school, I moved to the state of Alabama—a state that I know of as a state with great racial and homophobic intent. I thought that this move would be a great restart for me. My parents wanted to make the move because the state of Illinois was too "democratic" for them, and Alabama was more "conservative" and held the "Christian values" that my parents did. I will never forget my first week of freshman year of high school. The third day I showed up with a pink polo and khaki shorts, and I had on an arm sling because I greatly sprained my left shoulder. I was sitting in my math class in third period and watched as all the jocks would stare at me with the "limp wrist" and would repeat things that I would say in conversation with other students. From that point on, I knew that it would be a rough four years. I remember being told by my closest friends in high school that I was not allowed to come to their houses because their parents did not believe in my "lifestyle of choice." That one statement always shakes me to my very core. Why would someone choose a lifestyle that would lead others to tell them to "go kill themselves" or even be subjected to bodily harm? The statement of it being a "choice" is illogical. My biggest fans in high school were always the sports players. When we had to discuss topics for group projects or I would ask a question, I always received a tense, short response that was delivered by a contorted countenance. My nickname given to me by the baseball team—and you will get a kick out of it—was the "n***** fa****;" I thought it to be quite an inventive name, it must have taken a long time for them to come up with it, I mean, they only had three years to come up with it (this was in my junior year). I was friends with all the girls that the baseball players were either dating or head-over-heels for; not a single one of them scorned them or rose to say something when they hurled that term. No matter who I was friends within high school, I knew that no one ever truly had my back, because let's face the facts: there were only five Black people in my high school, and I was the only one in a class of 215. In high school, the only things that I was known for was always having one of the highest GPAs in my grade and being a good trumpet player. People would always ask, "are you going to be the Black Albert Einstein?" Or "are you going to be the next Louis Armstrong?" These questions were because they were impressed, but simply because I am Black. None of them ever thought about the potential implications of the questions they asked. Many of the teachers at Ardmore High School knew of the things that the aforementioned students did, but because the students were either popular or good sports-players, none of them said a thing. It was then that I realize how truly ingrained racism and homophobic views were in southern society. I silently fought a lot of battles at school and loudly fought battles at home. Even though my father was Black, he was very white-washed. He greatly despised the Black community and very deeply detested the LGBTQ+ community—he dubbed them all "booty boys." He was a very racist and intolerant man. If someone wasn't Christian or a republican conservative, he was always trying to aggressively change their point-of-view or greatly scorn them. In all honesty, my father was just a disturbed Vietnam War veteran with severe PTSD and health issues and was extremely mad at the world for inherent reasons. I could not come home and talk about my issues out of pure fear of being harmed or kicked out. My parents would swear up and down to the outside world that they would never do anything to harm their kids, but state records of known child abuse would beg to differ. Digressing from the home issues, one of my most vivid memories was sitting at a bonfire my junior year of high school for band. One of my friend's sister was questioning me about why I am gay and when did I decide that. Upon giving terse responses, one of the graduating seniors said, "Are you comfortable with knowing you are going to Hell? I cannot agree with your lifestyle." I was silent after that point as I was trying to hold back my tears. After the bonfire my best friend at the time asked me what was the matter, and after describing what happened, her response was, "I'm sorry they said those things, but I agree with them. You are my friend, but I will never agree with your lifestyle." This moment really solidified the notion that I was alone in my struggle, and I went through high school, to the day I graduated, living that truth.

Basic Combat Training and the Kennesaw State University Chapter

After high school, I went through basic combat training (BCT) in Fort Jackson, SC. I consider this point in my life as the turning point for me. I was surrounded by many people that did not care that I was gay or Black, because at the end of the day, we all made the oath to support and defend the Constitution of the United Stated from all enemies, foreign and domestic; this means that there might come a time where we will give our lives for each other, and each and every one of us cherished this notion. After BCT, I went to Little Creek, VA for advanced individual training (AIT). Here I was amongst fellow musicians, and quite a few of them were of the LGBTQ+ community; I fit in and it was a whole new experience for me. The Commandant of Training was the US Army Major that had his same-sex wedding posted on the front of the Army Times Magazine in 2013—a time before bans were lifted on same-sex marriage. That major was a hero to me and showed that no matter what the outside thinks, it is your life and you must life it your way. After AIT I started my first semester at KSU, that semester was a culture shock. I had never experienced being amongst so many Black students. I felt as if I didn't fit in because I went to mostly white schools and had never been around others that looked like me. I felt as if I was white washed myself, but three particular students at KSU helped me find my identity and to this day, I am proud to be a gay Black musician. My charge to whomever is reading this is to find who you are and be proud, do not let others dictate how you should dress or talk. Live your life according to how you want to live it; at the end of the day, it will always be your life and you will always know YOUR TRUTH.

To My Own Beat

Stephanie N Phillips

Growing up in a family where only half of us weremusically inclined was hard when I began first playing classical percussion and drum set. I didn't have any references on what to listen to or who to study with. My goal was never to play music professionally or study it, I honestly thought about going pro in the WNBA while I was younger and becoming a detective simultaneously somehow. When I finally made the decision to study music seriously, I realized that I was not represented well in the music I studied. Majority of the ensembles I played in consisted of white students for the most part with 2 or 3 Black students. Most of them ended up being Black men, and while it was great to see Black people occupying that space in general, I would've thrived even more seeing a Black woman take the stage.

I remained in my hometown for my undergrad degree and I remember going to my first rehearsal at a professional gig and the percussion section was nothing but older white men. The looks they gave me when I walked into the section could've been framed and put on display. It was bad enough that I was Black but was ALSO a woman. They assumed I couldn't perform well until I was given the chance to play and their faces were lit up in seconds. My appearance simply made me unworthy of being a part of an experience that these white men thought belonged to them. Those cold looks made me start to doubt myself anywhere that I went to play music. I felt as if I had to prove myself to these white people and that if I messed up or did not perform well that I failed. Honestly, it was just me being human and making the mistakes I needed to make in order to grow as a musician.

When I moved to Philadelphia to pursue my master's in Jazz Performance, I found a mentor who was also a drummer, and he assured me that being a part of this music (Jazz) was my right and my ancestors paved the way for me. Jazz is Black American Music (BAM), and still there are white people that think they run this. I've heard some of my fellow white male music colleagues talk about one another as if they aren't all still learning to play this music. This music is a lifetime learning process and to think you could learn it in 4 years is ridiculous. The Jazz bands I also played in were swarmed with white men who thought they knew jazz because they could play a run by John Coltrane or Miles Davis. When in fact Jazz is much more than notes, it's a cultural experience that Black people understand best because it is what our ancestors left for us.

I have learned much on my musical journey including how to be patient. I am becoming the musician I've always wanted to be and I am going to help the students that are in the same position to see themselves in a good way, while learning any type of music. What drew me to classical music was the way composers wrote for large ensembles while keeping everyone in mind during the compositions. Some are very slow and beautiful that make you want to cry, and others convey a mood of victory, such as a Sousa march. Jazz on the other hand makes you feel like getting on the dance floor. My teacher always says "if the crowd ain't moving then the song isn't happening." Jazz is very expressive and anyone can create their own sound, all while stealing from the greats that came before us such as, Ellington, Basie, Davis, Coltrane, Parker, and many more.

Becoming a teacher is something I've always believed would help me make my impact on the future of music. When you see someone who looks like you doing the things you want to do, it reassures you that you can make it in this field too. Being Black in music should be a positive experience in any setting and not threatening or fearful. We belong here in these institutions just as much as anyone else.

Do They Really Want Me?

Jeremiah Robinson

I have known for a long time that I wanted to go into the arts. When I was young, I would tell everyone I wanted to go to Julliard, not even fully knowing what that meant. My senior year, it started getting serious — I started filling out applications for schools and signing up for auditions. I did not realize how much work, time, and money it would take for auditions and applications. It was getting close to audition times, and I was getting overwhelmed rehearsing for my last musical, getting ready for choral competitions and my auditions, doing schoolwork and working 25 hours a week. When talking about this on multiple occasions, someone would always say to me,

"You will be fine, all schools are always looking for Black boys."

I never quite understood why anyone would say that to me, however, I know they were saying that in a way to make me feel better. There are so many things to unpack in that small sentence. At the time, I was looking to major in musical theatre. For major musical theatre schools, they would make big announcements about who was accepted that year, so it was easy to find pictures of people who were accepted to the schools in years past. I went through and found all the accepted classes, specifically to see if there were any Black people there. Out of the twenty —give or take—students that were accepted every year, these schools would only accept about two or three Black students. This was very discouraging; I wanted to see whether they were diverse in their choices or if they were just looking for a "token". This takes me back to the phrase

"You will be fine; all schools are always looking for Black boys."

Are they looking for Black talent or just someone to fill their quota? Comments like this encourage imposter syndrome in a lot of Black performers.

I ended up starting college later that year. The first semester, I started as a musical theatre major and while I had fun, I still heard the same phrase,

"You are going to be so successful, people are always looking for Black performers."

Is that really the only reason you believe I will be successful? This is what made me doubt myself. This seems like a harmless phrase to most people, but I wonder why? How would you feel if someone said, "They will love you, everyone loves white girls!" It belittles the work we have done. There were many times where I felt like I have afforded many of the opportunities only because I am Black, but I know that I have had to work twice as hard as my lighter counterparts. I know I deserve every opportunity I have been given, that is why I have chosen to become a music educator, to encourage Black students like me. To constantly remind them that being the "token" is not your assignment in this world. You are not only wanted, but needed in this world!

Mrs. Micro-Aggression

Alissa Gittens

I remember the first time I was an adjudicator for Solo and Ensemble Festival in our state. To say I was excited was an understatement. A few years of engaging with the community, its music educators, and their students fueled my desire to support the district in fairly adjudicating student musicians while offering words of encouragement. I was intent about the positive impact I wanted to impart on these young flutists.

When I arrived for check in at the site, the school's cafeteria, I estimated there were approximately 100 music educators in the room. The sea of music educators consisted mostly of middle aged to older white males with a slightly lower representation of white females, followed by a sprinkle of Black men and one handful of Black women. In an instant, I realized that I did not look the part of a "traditional" adjudicator.

My youthful disposition often makes me the target for ageism by some disgruntled veteran educators whose deeply rooted biases view me as underqualified or incompetent because of how young they perceive me to be. On one too many occasions during brief introductions, these perpetrators were emboldened to interrogate me about the integrity of my music degree from a historically Black college they know little about while simultaneously posturing themselves with highlights of their career achievements. I cannot help but to wonder if their cynicism is a result of my Blackness. This routine internal debate is the result of my experiences as a Black flutist in under-melanated classical performance spaces. The events of the day were another unfortunate confirmation of my suspicion.

Luckily, I saw some familiar faces who greeted me with smiles and hugs. The county music supervisor, who is also a friend, introduced me to two other flute adjudicators. Already seated at the table, was a middle-aged white woman and a seemingly older Black woman. We exchanged pleasantries for a moment before being escorted to our assigned classrooms.

As I walked through the hall, an unfamiliar older white woman approached me to introduce herself. Apparently, she knew who I was without introduction. My greeting began with an apology because I did not know her and she seemed eager to address me. She explained that her former middle school band member was currently my private student. I confirmed that I was the instructor once she mentioned the student's name. She then patronizingly asserted, "You know… (student's name) has such a strong work ethic, but poor child, he really has no talent at all."

Once my brain processed her tasteless remarks, I immediately froze in disbelief. The doors to our classrooms were steps away and were crowded with parents and anxious students. Before I could gather myself to address her inappropriate remarks, she patted my shoulder, wished me luck, and walked into her room locking the door behind her.

The Taurean bull in me wanted to bust the door open to read her for filth, but my hyper-vigilant Blackness knew that I could not approach her with such intense emotions absent of any consequences of swift judgement from bystanders. There was a line of students and protective parents/guardians glaring at me as they were ready to begin their adjudication, and were not interested in my feelings in that moment. There was no time to sort my thoughts. My emotions were high, but I had to stifle them in order to be of service to the young musicians present. Many questions arose while I processed the interaction as the minutes passed:

How could an educator make remarks about a student in such a degrading manner?

Why did she think it was appropriate to address me upon our first ever interaction with her criticism?

What was her intention?

What was it about my presence that allowed her to feel empowered and speak so disparagingly about a child? Did she know she was wrong?

Did she even care?

During the first break of the morning, I promptly walked to her classroom with hopes of addressing the issue, but she was not there. The opportunity to admonish her unprofessional behavior never presented itself again for the remainder of the day. The demeaning encounter marred my first experience as an adjudicator.

I had mixed emotions on whether I should inform my student's parents of the unfortunate exchange at Solo and Ensemble Festival. Days later, I had a scheduled lesson with the student who for the record is African-American. With great hesitance, I chose to inform the parents of what transpired. They were angry! According to the parents, this act of racism in the form of a micro-aggression was not the first incident involving their child and unfortunately not likely to be the last.

Initially, the parents were discontent with me because they believed I did not defend their child's honor. I talked them through their emotions and discussed the likelihood of his presence being devalued again in white spaces, especially in classical music. I encouraged them to avoid telling their child about the incident in order to protect his self-esteem and not diminish his passion for flute performance.

My students deserve to experience the world of music free of bigoted stereotypes and the burden of being beautifully Black in white spaces where they are likely to be out-numbered by race and unconsciously underestimated. Whom else did that irresponsible educator influence over the last few decades with her problematic behavior? How many other students did she deflate with her toxic core beliefs?

The same microaggressions I suffered as a child 30 plus years ago are haunting my students today. I often feel despondent as a result. Why do Black musicians still have to deal with such careless treatment in performing art spaces? I just want to be a flutist. I simply want my Black students to experience the joy of music without racist acts by insecure and emotionally immature adults.

There was never an opportunity for me to address or absolve the hurt of this incident and others like it. Rarely is there ever an opportunity for closure. I am still angry. Nonetheless, I refuse to remain complicit with the pervasive culture of Eurocentrism in music education. I have begun doing the work to create safe and collaborative spaces for flutists across the African Diaspora. I have turned my experiences of "othering" into a community of inclusivity by centering BIPOC (Black, Indigenous, and People of color) in The Urban Flautistas Fest and the Flutists of Color group on Facebook. I pray that young flutists of color can experience the joy of music making while maintaining their childhood innocence without the gatekeepers of racism in the performing arts disrupting their journey.

P.S.
My "no talent" student has since graduated from a conservatory as a music performance major and is pursuing graduate studies.

I Don't Sing Like That

Nasia Shayne

At the age of six, my mother sat me down at the creaky bench of the old upright piano, explaining that my younger sister and I "are not going to sit on our asses and do nothing after school—we will learn an instrument and play a sport."

As the lessons started, I grew fond of the soft, ivory flesh that replaced my delicate fingertips and became an extension of me; I craved the moments where we could sit together and create a universe of music and life that was only inhabited by me and the spirit of song. This is where I would develop a confidence, love, and desire for music that seemed impenetrable; my world would become doused in a rosy glow of peace and tolerance. Some children get to experience the world as the vast field of exploration and creativity that it is supposed to be, however, the rose-colored glasses are removed at some point for us all. In most instances, for Black children living in America, it is ripped from us much more quickly and violently. We are forced to grow up and deal with the harsh realities of life at young ages due to historical abuse and gaslighting from society, institutionalized racism and segregation that plagues American society, and extreme trauma. My parents attempted to ensure that my sister and

I would be able to live our lives only worrying about half of these, but that does not prevent the inevitable. The bubble will burst. That young artist who was convinced that the world would never be cruel or shatter her love for music, would one day realize that her love for music would change over time at the hands of institutionalized bias and racism. Her confidence would be shattered and never restored to its original radiance. That perfect universe she engulfed herself in daily would be shattered with a single thought that would then haunt her for the rest of her career in music.

I don't sing like that.

My mother put us in singing lessons soon after. She wanted us to be the next MaryMary[1]. I grew up listening to a mix of their music, Yolonda Adams[2], Curt Carr[3], and other Gospel singers, but favored the Hillsong[4], the Plus One[5], the Selah[6], the contemporary Christian singers who sounded nothing like the earthy Gospel singers my parents' favored. It truly was only because it was simpler, the melodies and harmonies easier for my young brain to grasp. I sang along in the car or around the house, carefree and full of passion.

1 Mary Mary is a female American urban contemporary gospel duo composed of sisters Erica Atkins-Campbell and Trecina Atkins-Campbell.
2 Yolanda Yvette Adams is an American gospel singer, record producer, actress, and host of her own nationally syndicated morning gospel show.
3 Kurt Carr is an American gospel music composer and performer.
4 A contemporary Chirsitian church founded by Brian and Bobby Huston in 1983. HIllsong writes and performs Chistian contemporary music.
5 Christian music's early millennium answer to secular acts such as N*SYNC and Backstreet Boys, Plus One was an American Christian pop boy band.
6 Selah was originally formed by brother and sister, Todd and Nicol Smith. They became known for transforming old Christian hymns into a more modern style and with their powerful voices and beautiful harmonies.

I noticed, though, that when I would attempt to sing along with the ballads of Amy Grant[7], I would get substantially less judgment from others on my tone than when I would attempt to sing the gospel songs. It wasn't until I was selected for the talent show at my all-white, Christian private school where I was expected—better yet, required—to sing a Gospel song, that it became painstakingly obvious. I chose to sing "Victory" by Yolonda Adams because it was my favorite song. Yolanda sang with such fire and gusto that I was sure I also had packed in my ten-year-old body. I climbed onto the stage alone, only slightly aware of the crowd of people watching, and began to sing. I looked for my parents' faces, and while they were smiling, a child can tell when they have not met their parents' unspoken expectations.

The expectation for me, a Black kid, is to sing a gospel song well on instinct, to be sassy, to not speak well, to cover up, to sit still, to speak quietly, to be athletic, to love fried chicken and watermelon, to have only one parent, to be angry, and to fulfill every stereotype out there. Fact is, I cannot eat chicken on the bone because the veins freak me out. I'm only considered sassy because I speak my mind and most can't handle it. I have breasts that have been over-sexualized since I was nine. I've given up code-switching[8] since no matter what I will be viewed as the angry Black woman instead of passionate. My parents are together, educated, have served in the military and have been there for every event in my life yet will only be viewed as Black first. My knees suck so running hurts and I have lost my athletic gusto since middle school. I cannot sit still to save my life. I'm angry as hell. I cannot sing Gospel as an untrained 10 year-old.

7 Amy Lee Grant is an American singer, songwriter and musician. She has been referred to as "The Queen of Christian Pop."

In addition to the humiliation this performance brought, it also exposed a crisis in me that had hidden itself until that moment. I'm Black, but not enough, but also too much, but tolerable. 'I like you because you aren't ghetto.' I was six. 'You speak so well.' How else am I supposed to speak? 'You're pretty for a Black girl.' Bless your heart[9]. 'I like that you don't have a wobbly voice.' Girl you mean vibrato[10]???

'Why do you sing like that?'

I want to know the same damn thing so let me know when you find out…

I digress... After the show, I was ridiculed for how I was nothing like a gospel performer and sang blandly 'like those white people', and the overwhelming and panicked thought arose inside of me. I must not have sang well if I didn't sound like her. Right? I'm not Black enough because I don't sing like an adult woman at ten.

I don't sing like that.

Growing up being the only Black kid everywhere I went impacted my view of myself as an individual and as a musician. I was the only Black sixth-grade girl at my small Private School in Kennesaw, Georgia and was expected, again, to do two things: sing and play sports. I was the MVP

8 Code-switching as it's been coined by the POC community—specifically centered around the Black experience—is when Black people switch the way they speak, act, and interact with colleagues within their jobs.

9 An insult commonly used in the south.

10 A rapid, slight variation in pitch in singing or playing some musical instruments, producing a stronger or richer tone.

in basketball and a leader in my choir. Everyone was happy when I was doing either one of those and excelling. When I wanted to cheer, my white coach publicly humiliated and yelled at me (until I was in tears) about how I was a ballplayer and 'not a wimpy cheerleader' and I was not made for that. Why can't Black girls be soft and dainty too? When I wanted to quit chorus and try a different elective but felt uncomfortable speaking honestly with the white choir director who constantly made suggestive comments about her students of color, I was cornered by two adults alone and told that I 'was a liar and not dependable because I was letting choir down' and 'would be punished by God for sitting on my gifts'. Why can't Black girls be afraid too?

At the age of twelve, I knew that white people expected one thing out of me: to perform. Not just in the fine arts, but I had to excel at all things in order to be appreciated and respected as an individual. This is where I perfected the art of Code Switching. I got a perm, I begged my mom for the expensive garb the other white girls had, and intentionally removed myself from anything that would classify me as "ghetto." I was not allowed the opportunity to know myself because it had been laid out for me. I was the MVP and Captain. I was the Scholar; the polite student. I was the Choir Geek. I was the respectable one. I was "easy to swallow." I was the quiet one. I put on a good show. See, I was the token in every situation. I had been my whole life, and I had no one to guide me through it. This caused a storm in me that only fueled the screaming voice that insisted that I was not enough. I was depressed, anxious, self-deprecating, and insecure. I was a leader in every situation but I was convinced I was undeserving, not qualified, and chosen out of pity or out of a need to meet a requirement. It should not be me even though I worked hard for the titles I held. An identity crisis raged through me, and code switching made it impossible to recognize which version of me was truly me anymore. The only thing I knew was that people preferred the 'tolerable' version of me, and I so desperately needed to please people. So, instead of fighting back and pursuing my interests, dreams, and curiosity, I wiped my eyes, looked the adults in the eye, and performed, while the burning embers that rested in my pit hissed...

But I don't sing like that.

At this point, I would be remiss to mention mental health in the Black community. As a depressed middle schooler, I had a difficult time getting the help I needed due to the beliefs that circulate through the Black community concerning mental health. We don't talk about our household issues outside the house. You don't do that white people shit. You're following that stupid anxiety fad. My parents were terrified and dealing with their own emotions and experience, and my situation was not handled well. It was not until college that I was able to get the help that I needed. There is an unspoken narrative in the Black community that therapy and mental health assistance is 'for white people' and not something that we should access. We are supposed to be strong willed and push it down, push through it, overcome. We cannot ask for help because we don't need anything from "them". Even if we had understanding and 'progressive' support systems, there are other challenges to face. Not only is it a battle against stereotypes and biases, but it is simply not affordable for all people. It is expensive to be sick, physically and mentally, and often, mental health is ignored because it's unseen. It is not

obvious or in your face, which means that it is not taken as seriously.
Unfortunately, to admit that we are struggling mentally is to appear weak. People who are mentally ill are shunned and social pariahs. So it is not surprising that when I was officially diagnosed with

High functioning Anxiety Disorder[18], Panic Disorder[19], and Moderate Depression, I retreated into myself and was determined to hide this new incriminating quality of myself. This was something new to hate, a new 'something different' to obsess over, another reason to believe that I was not worthy of success because I did not have a "normal brain." A new them v. me that gave them a better advantage, because even if they struggled too, help was way more easy to access for them.

I don't sing like that.

I went to a reputable Performing Arts High School in the area and from the first day I was the oddball. I was no longer in suburbia, but in a more 'urban' part of the district. The program was embedded in a traditional school, and there was a distinct segregation between who we deemed as the PA (performing arts) kids and the District (students who were zoned for the school) kids. The PA kids were placed in all honors classes, had the most concessions, were seemingly untouchable by the actual deans and administrators, and were deeply irritating to the District kids. The district kids

10 Typically refers to someone who experiences anxiety while still managing daily life quite well.
11 An anxiety disorder characterized by unexpected and repeated episodes of intense fear accompanied by physical symptoms that may include chest pain, heart palpitations, shortness of breath, dizziness, or abdominal distress.

were mostly POC (people of color), who were painted as thugs and bad influences by the PA teachers. Any PA kid caught mingling with them would become a social pariah and avoided for fear of contacting the trouble maker label from the adults. The majority of the Performing Arts (PA) Program white kids. In addition to the battle of race and ethnicity, there was the battle of money.

Some parents bought their students lead roles through donations or hours spent in the costume room or a trip to a Disney Competition in return for a shining solo for their daughter. For the "average" PA student, this was not the reality, and a vicious competitiveness was born. Having enough money was the biggest advantage, being white was just a plus. If you had both, you were golden.

God forbid if you were Black. You were either assumed a district, or needed to be tamed. In my case, my parents both worked, attended school, and we were not able to donate hundreds of thousands of dollars to the program or contribute any time working in the costume room with the other gossipy moms, so I had to perform and compete based on talent alone. The transition to this school and environment was the biggest shock of my life. I was no longer the token. I was lost in a sea of Black faces that all looked like mine. This should have comforted me, as now I had time to relax, but it became a source of anxiety for me. I was not expected to perform in the same way, where I would be expected to be featured for the sake of "inclusivity" and "sensitivity" or because it was expected of me as a Black kid. Everyone looked like me. I had to, again, overperform to even be acknowledged, let alone considered, and even then barely. The sad reality is that there were some talented kids that sang, danced, acted their asses off and who were geniuses in technical theater that genuinely deserved the hype and others that were constantly overlooked. That school was overflowing with talent, on both sides (district and PA), but still, there was the star group, the face of the school. It was mostly white, wealthy, and exclusive with a few token people of color. During my time there, I had not seen one hispanic student take any leads, and saw only a handful of Black students shine. And even though I was excluded from the elite, I found myself daily craving their status, craving what they had and working to be that way and work my way into the eyes of my teachers and shine. I mastered the art of Code Switching. In my PA classes, I was respectable, sang anything but gospel for official classes, covered up, kept quiet, and played nice with people who were in the "In Crowd". I thought that would be the key to success. But I can't dance for shit. I am too passive for acting (but if I was passionate, I became too aggressive instantly). I was not wealthy. I was not passionate enough. I was not white and thin.

I don't sing like that.

This enraged me. How could it be, that we are not the minority, and we are still fighting for even a simple acknowledgment? I had worked hard to get where I was. I studied and was respectful, I did the work and was always passed over. It was impossible and day after day, I was always shown why white was right and preferred. I had to find flesh-tone character shoes (an out of pocket expense), but the deep brown ones didn't match me because I was Black and that was all they had to offer for Black people at the time. I had to wear my hair back for concerts and it was never worn natural because that was too distracting. The only time my

Black best friend at the time got a lead was when she was playing an Ape in Tarzan. During class, I was expected to sit, sing well, retain information, and perform. Shut up and perform. The only place I could find peace was the Gospel Choir, facilitated by the only Black music teacher there. Our Gospel Choir was made up of anyone who wanted to sing, and whoever prepared the solo got the solo. Yet, the Gospel Choir was not able to perform at the normal choir events. They were only reserved for outside performances that were coordinated by our teacher or by ourselves, and the Black history month show. Even our incredible band that followed an HBCU band style was not even considered a part of the magnet program. If it was because all these things were "too Black" or "too preachy", who knows, but all I knew is that we were not welcome in the PA world and not seen as "truly talented".

It is ironic, because the out crowd was where I found my voice as a leader and experimented as a singer. My role as a confident leader started and stopped every Tuesday and Thursday after school. During class, it was a choral tone with no vibrato and conformity. Even when we had an opportunity for class projects, where we were able to sing a solo song, we were only allowed to pick a musical theater song or classical art song. There was always a reason not to do the Black created and inspired shows too. Gershwin[12] or Art Songs[13]. And so, after a year and a half of attempting to sing like myself, I gave

12 George Gershwin, original name Jacob Gershvin, (September 26, 1898—July 11, 1937, Hollywood, California), was one of the most significant and popular American composers of all time. He wrote primarily for theBroadway musical theatre, but as well as orchestral and piano compositions in which he blended, in varying degrees, the techniques and forms of classical music with the stylistic nuances and techniques of popular music and jazz.

13 A song written to be sung in recital, typically with piano accompaniment and often set to a poem.

into it and started to conform. I stripped myself of any flare, and sang exactly like they wanted me to.

I don't sing like that.

I've always loved listening to people sing spirituals[14], but I hate preparing and performing them. This hatred grew deeper in college. I have never sat down, in a choral rehearsal or setting, and spoken freely and deeply about the meanings behind the haunting words that are spirituals. I have sung plenty since I was a child, some too many times over and some not enough. There was never an educating moment for the audience on why we, a mostly white choir, were singing a song written by slaves to end our masterfully programmed performance? I was told once that it was to 'leave the audience with a good note'. Yes, songs that were written to bring ease and hope to a stolen, raped, abused, tormented, and lost people sung by white folk definitely only exists as a big finish at the end of your white washed concert. I ask now, what is that good note? That we are inclusive because we sang one Black song? Or that we sang it at the end so the audience knows that we are inclusive and diverse? Or because they are fun and upbeat? Or because we are so far removed from Slavery and Segregation that we can celebrate on it and look back on it with golden sparkly lenses? During my undergraduate studies, we sang a Gospel Mass[15]. I loved the beautiful work, but was furious at the end of every rehearsal. To be frank, it was white washed. The Black students would protest and

14 A religious song of a kind associated with Black Christians of the southern US, and thought to derive from the combination of European hymns and African musical elements by Black slaves.

15 Mass (religion), the ritual of chants, readings, prayers, and other ceremonies used in. the celebration of the Eucharist in the Roman Catholic church. The same name is used in high Anglican churches.

make suggestions on how to make it more authentic and it would fall on deaf ears. It was infuriating.The only relief I had was when the school's professor of African American Music came and did a master class. The music finally fell together and sounded like the gospel work it was intended to be. Yet, when presented, all of the gospel characteristics were stripped and we were left with a whitewashed mess once again. I think of that concert and cringe to this day. I truly cannot enjoy the work without a tinge of lingering resentment. Here we are, Black people, explaining how to sing our music, and are told that it is wrong and undesirable unless it is sung the white-right-way. It is our music. It is not to be performed that way. It is to be spoken about and dissected and sung with empathy and emotion. This is the Black experience. Every aspect of Black culture has been taken and appropriated from us. Music. Culture. Labor. Hair. Our hair is only the tip of the iceberg. From the Kardashians trying to brand and trademark braided hairstyles that are historically ours to people trying to justify dreadlocks v. matted locs. We are constantly told that our culture is wrong for us, but okay to be stolen. I have to question the professionalism of my hair daily, yet it is in the latest fashion trends that people can wear for a weekend and remove in time for work. It does not make sense. I'm wrong. I'm not right. I'm not White and can't get away with it.

I don't sing like that.

You would think the performing arts world would be more accepting right? I had never seen or heard of a queer performer until I got to college. I came out in high-school to a couple of friends, but I had no intention on making anything public due to the initial fear or eternal damnation and rejection from my family, but the idea that if I were to come public as a queer woman, I would never get a job. Even as I was pursuing my degree in Music Education, I was often told "If you want to get a job in *insert very rich, desirable area to teach in here*, you are going to have to be in the closet for a few years" or to "keep your private life private." So not only was I supposed to box in the teachings of music and ostracize the beautiful masterpieces created by Black musicians, I now also have to ignore the queer ones as well? Black queer children are homeless and Black, trans women are being murdered left and right, and I could be the only safe place for a student if they only knew they could relate to me, but I was not allowed to be even this part of myself either?

When I was in college, I was forced to wear this horrid choir dress that was unflattering and made me all over uncomfortable in my own body. When I requested to wear a tux just as the conductor did, I was told that it would disrupt the uniform and would stand out and was not supposed to.

Then Ahmaud Aubrey[16]. Then Trayvon Martin[17]. Then Breonna Taylor[18]. Then George Floyd[19]. Then Emmitt Till[20]. Then Vanessa Guillen[21]. Then the children in cages[22]. Then Elijah McCain[23]. Then Eric Garner[24]. Then Flint, Michigan[25]. Then Dakota Access Pipeline protests[26]. Then the Black Lives Matter Protests[27]. Then the countless names forgotten in the massacre of a people based on something so irreversible as the color of skin. Then the continuous injustices against people of color everywhere. Then I got fed the fuck up. Then I decided to do something and be an active agent of change.

I coordinated a small protest during the summer of 2020 with some colleagues of mine, and had added my university's name to the flyer, and was immediately contacted and asked to remove the name. Why? They did not want to be associated with violence and unrest for fear or losing donors.

They would rather turn a blind eye and keep money than stand for injustice. That is not uncommon. In fact, it is expected. Injustice occurs. We let it slide and it happens again and again and again. We get fed up and do something about it. We are told to shut up and perform.

16 February 23, 2020, Ahmaud Arbery, a 25-year-old Black man, was murdered during a racially-motivated hate crime while jogging in Satilla Shores, a neighborhood near Brunswick in Glynn County, Georgia.
17 Trayvon Benjamin Martin was a 17-year-old African-American boy from Miami Gardens, Florida, who was fatally shot in Sanford, Florida by George Zimmerman, a 28-year-old Hispanic American.
18 Breonna Taylor, a 26-year-old African-American woman, was fatally shot in her Louisville, Kentucky, apartment on March 13, 2020, when at least seven police officers forced entry into the apartment as part of an investigation into drug dealing operations.
19 George Perry Floyd Jr. was an African-American man who was murdered by a police officer in Minneapolis, Minnesota, during an arrest after a store clerk suspected Floyd may have used a counterfeit twenty-dollar bill, on May 25, 2020.
20 Emmett Louis Till was a 14-year-old African American boy who was abducted, tortured and lynched in Mississippi in 1955, after being accused of offending a white woman in her family's grocery store.
21 The murder of Vanessa Guillén, a 20-year-old United States Army soldier, took place inside an armory at Fort Hood, Texas, on April 22, 2020, when she was bludgeoned to death by another soldier, Aaron David Robinson. Guillén had been missing for over two months when some of her dismembered remains were found buried along the Leon River on June 30.
22 The government has endangered the health of children by separating families and children from each other, caging children in unsanitary and unsafe conditions, and has pro- posed detaining children indefinitely.

I was in my apartment parking lot at the end of a long, exhausting day of student teaching, sobbing on the phone with my now wife when I came to a life changing conclusion: I'm tired of this shit and I do not want to be a musician anymore. Some might say tiredness won the battle against my grit, and 'quitting' invalidates everything I've just stated before. I did not stop being a musician because I am afraid of scrutiny, or judgment, or the opinions and expectations of white people. If I wanted to escape that, I would frankly be dead, as there is no escaping that. I stopped singing because if I were to continue, there would be no more musicianship left in me. It would have snuffed out every last drop of love and adoration for music that was left, and I did not want to even risk them taking that from me too. I no longer wanted to sing like that, or like them. I wanted to sing like me.

As my Grandfather always told me, the only thing I can do is be Black and die, so why the hell was I so set on pleasing white people who are going to find an issue with me anyway? I was tired of conforming. Tired of holding back. Tired of

23 Elijah Jovan McClain was a 23-year-old Black American massage therapist from Aurora, Colorado, who died after a violent police encounter.

24 On July 17, 2014, Eric Garner was killed in the New York City borough of Staten Island after Daniel Pantaleo, a New York City Police Department (NYPD) officer, put him in a prohibited chokehold while arresting him.

25 The Flint water crisis was a public health crisis that started in 2014 and lasted until 2019, after the drinking water for the city of Flint, Michigan was contaminated with lead and possibly Legionella bacteria.

26 The Dakota Access Pipeline Protests, also called by the hashtag #NoDAPL, began in early 2016 as a grassroots opposition to the construction of Energy Transfer Partners' Dakota Access Pipeline in the northern United States. The pipeline runs from the Bakken oil fields in western North Dakota to southern Illinois, crossing beneath the Missouri and Mississippi rivers, as well as under part of Lake Oahe near the Standing Rock Indian Reservation. Many members of the Standing Rock tribe and surrounding communities consider the pipeline to

holding onto the persona of someone who I was never meant to be. I never really denied my Blackness, but for a long time, I was taught to be ashamed of it and to hide aspects of it in my song. I reject fears of not being accepted and the idea of 'not being good enough'. I was taught to be embarrassed by my voice. I speak up unashamedly. I was taught that my tone was wrong because I wasn't born a natural born gospel singer. Not everyone was meant to be. I was taught that I had to scrape my way up to be noticed. I will be noticed where I am needed and celebrated where I am appreciated. I was taught that I was supposed to take up little space. I am meant to live loud, vibrant and without limits. I was taught that I would have to work harder than everyone else to get the bare minimum. I will no longer accept the bare minimum for the work I put out and will not tolerate disrespect towards myself as an artist or my work. I was taught to shut up and take scraps and bare minimum effort. I will not accept anything less than accurate effort and excellence when it comes to my heritage and history- anything else is an insult.

I was taught to perform, but I don't sing like that.

be a serious threat to the region's water. The construction also directly threatens ancient burial grounds and cultural sites of historic importance.

27 Black Lives Matter is a decentralized political and social movement that seeks to highlight racism, discrimination, and inequality experienced by Black people. When its supporters come together, they do so primarily to protest incidents of police brutality and racially motivated violence against Black people.

A Path Chosen

Robyn Smith

In the fall of 2021, I moved to Chicago and started my first professional orchestra appointment as the second trombonist of the Michigan Opera Theater. I decided to move to Chicago after finishing my Master's degree at NEC[1] because I felt it was the perfect city to expand my career. I wanted the opportunity to hear the Chicago Symphony weekly, work with organizations like Chicago Music Pathways Initiative[2], and be amongst some of this country's most talented Black artists. There is an important story of how I got to this point. For the first time in my life I am able to choose the environment I inhabit, the spaces I'd like to work in and the artists I wish to collaborate with. Black artists must be strategic about the spaces they occupy in order to not only survive, but thrive in this field. The Black artist's story is unique from the colleagues that surround us. Our culture and needs become apparent as we enter predominantly white spaces. The path I chose is led and directly affected by my upbringing.

1 The New England Conservatory of Music.

2 As written on their website, an organization with a mission to "increase diversity in America's professional, musical landscape, and particularly in its orchestras, promoting equity, vibrancy, and sustainability within those organizations and the extraordinary art form they celebrate." https://chicagopathways.org.

A Family Affair

I remember being excited about tagging along with my Dad to take my brother Brandon to his drum lessons every Saturday. Thinking about those moments, I'm unsure if it was the Long John Silvers that I was sure to get or supporting my brother that I was excited about. Still, I know these early memories shaped my perception of what it took to hone a craft, particularly music. When my brother would give up shotgun, I rode in the front seat on trips to his orchestra rehearsals, district band concerts, and Jazz band gigs. My dad was the equivalent of what some might call a "soccer mom", he was a "band dad". Everyone knew that if they needed a ride, they could ride with Mr.Smith. I became cordial with Brandon's musician friends, them knowing me as "Brandon's little sis," but little did I know I was getting to know my future colleagues in the classical music scene.

When I talk about my time in middle and high school, people are usually shocked to hear my experiences, mostly because my classmates and I shared a rare journey. Growing up in Atlanta, Georgia was extremely rewarding but I now realize how much of an impact it had on the projection of my career. Atlanta is known as one of the "Black Mecca's" in this country. This not only means that the city holds a leading role in Black history, arts, music, and food, but that "Black success" was most definitely not an anomaly. The mentality is, "you are greatness," that being Black inherently makes you great, or for lack of a better term "fye" (fire). In short, I was taught that the color of my skin made me beautiful, strong and courageous. I attended all Black public schools from K-12 and I remember the mottos we recited every morning and the music played on the intercom that uplifted and validated us. This environment helped little Robyn know that whatever she pursued, she could be the very best at it.

Stages in Music

My first memory of music was in Kindergarten. My music teacher Ms. Oden led us in tons of songs to sing along to, xylophones to bang on and recorders to blow more spit than air in. I remember enjoying music class so much that by fourth grade, Ms. Oden suggested that my friends and I audition for the elementary honor chorus. Fourth grade also meant that we had an opportunity to join the band. In the instrument petting zoo, I realized that everyone was choosing trumpet, clarinet, saxophone and drums, so I chose trombone. All of fourth and fifth grade I was playing in band class and going to honor chorus every week with my friends. From early on in my music journey, having friends in music just made the experience more rewarding. It also made me feel like I belonged in the space.

Middle school was one of the most important times in my life. I was taught both jazz and western classical traditions and I spent a significant amount of time honing both. It was also my first time understanding what the color of my skin meant to others that didn't share it.

One of the most influential people in my life was Robert Jeffrey. Robert Jeffrey was my middle school band director and a "school father" to so many that he taught. He is a man that embodies discipline, respect, consistency, and passion. Being mediocre was never an option for his students. When I arrived in his band room in sixth grade (with him already meeting me through my brother) saying that I wanted to switch to trumpet, he said, "look, we need more girls on trombone and if we get a full girl trombone section, I'll get Beyoncé to come to the school." Whether he was serious or not didn't matter because by the look in his eyes, I knew that he saw me doing really well with the trombone. Mr. Jeffrey taught us accountability and discipline. We were expected to come to school early to practice before classes, we scheduled our own student-led sectionals, we studied music theory and scales with him during the summer and worked on inventory. Mr. J was also a very honest man. It was he that explained to us that there was a story already written for us when we showed up to state and district auditions in Georgia. We had to present ourselves in a professional manner at all times to not give them a reason to think they could outplay us. We were aware that we didn't have the same resources as the white kids in metro Atlanta, but it didn't mean we weren't capable of being just as good.

In high school, the gaps in resources and funding in music school programs became more evident. Making All-State and district ensembles meant traveling to the outskirts of Atlanta and being a part of the small number of Black students that made it into these groups. Rehearsals and other festivals were held at swanky high schools with large band rooms and dozens of top of the line instruments. The students of these schools were typically first chair in the ensembles. My friends and I noticed these patterns even though they did not discourage us from auditioning and being in these ensembles. It seemed as if we were getting the short end of the stick, however; we were happy to have made it so far despite the disparities. In ninth grade, I auditioned and became a member of the Atlanta Symphony Orchestra's Talent Development program. The Talent Development

Program's mission is to change the face of US orchestras by funding and guiding the careers of Black/Latinx musicians. This program provided me with exposure, resources and access which put me on an even playing field with more affluent students. I had assistance traveling to music schools to take lessons before college auditions which allowed me the opportunity to go off to The New England Conservatory of Music to study Classical Trombone Performance.

A Spark of Purpose

I became connected and drawn to the movement of representation in high art and the dismantling of oppressive structures that keep classical music predominantly white. I was only one of four to five Black females in the entire school which left me feeling isolated at times. Going from an all Black space to a predominantly Asian and White community was quite the adjustment. I was forced to seek belonging within myself in order to stay afloat. I joined the Black Student Union board and it became my source of community and validation for most of my time at NEC. We had each other to lean on for support and a safe space. The microaggressions we experienced in the conservatory as a collective became topics of many conversations in the school's cafe and BSU meetings. Our main desire was to enrich the NEC community with our culture and to be acknowledged as a vital part of the school's history and current culture. We wanted to be seen and heard while curating events and opportunities for Black students to feel like they belonged. From this point on, I began to feel a deeper connection to who I am, what I represent and how this affects my career after graduation.

Diversion

It was during my Master's in the middle of a pandemic that I had the time to reflect deeply on my career. From the sudden attention to the unjust killings of my people, to the inconsiderate and narcissistic behavior from President Donald Trump, I entered a deep space of self reflection. Although I expected that being an orchestral Black female trombonist would present its challenges externally, I underestimated just how much pursuing this career could affect my identity internally. It is difficult to exist in this country as a Black person and not be constantly reminded of the economic and social disparities. Classical music further exacerbates these issues and becomes a direct reflection of what systemic inequality can cause.

Unlike ever before, this internal crisis caused me to re-examine my goals in this field and become extremely intentional. The crisis speaks to wanting success in a field that continues to remind us of the imbalance of resources and funds in minority communities. Classical music embodies an elite high art culture that has always excluded people of color. I was forced to be intentional about why I'm pursuing a career that isolates and disconnects me from who I am. For the first time because of COVID, I was studying classical music alone...alone in my parents' basement and I had not been able to feel passionate about classical music. There was no cafe to decompress in, there was not a friend nearby to vent to, and there was not a room full of Black classical musicians who could speak to my experience. It's just me... and Strauss, Mahler, Thomas Morley and William Byrd.

"What am I doing?"

I realized that I have somehow operated haphazardly when it comes to my goals in this career. Teaching and playing in an orchestra isn't enough. If playing in an orchestra is the only end goal, then I will continue to feed into the cycle of elitism. Yes, my identity as a Black female trombonist is enough to attract different eyes, however, those "eyes" will not last long. If the issues are systemic, then they can't be changed just by my presence on stage.

My musicianship has always been well- rounded and my love for my community has always been deep within me. It was time for me to allow my story and culture to truly shape me and my career. In short, my career goals are no longer one-dimensional and I see now that my path does not have to be either. If I continue this journey fulfilling the expectations of the white institution, it will not be enough to make a difference. The path of a typical classical musician (orchestral training/schooling to prepare for an orchestral job) only benefits white people. I will not be fulfilled by this path and my presence in this field will be just "to say she could do it".

Given these points, the next step in my career will not only match my personal needs as a musician of color, but help guide me on a more intentional path. I want to be involved in my community on a deeper level through teaching, mentoring and performance work. I want to continue to perform in an orchestra, but I also would like to expand my freelancing career to other genres because my musicianship expands beyond Western European music. The opportunity to be in a vibrant city with a plethora of arts organizations that align with my values, while being in close proximity to my first professional job is a dream. Without this reflective space, I'm not sure if my values as a musician would've come first, moreover, I'm not sure if I would've decided to move to Chicago. I wanted the community in which I was raised to somewhat reflect my post-graduate life. Having a Black community is important to my growth and connecting the dots to the change I want to see happen in this field. In essence, my reflective space called for a balance within myself that allows me to combine my culture and experiences to shape my path so that I can contribute to the direct impact of representation and systemic equity. Understanding how to unlearn Eurocentric/White cultures and practices liberated me from chasing goals that will continue to feed the cycle of white supremacy. The stories of Black musicians/artists are too nuanced and complex to expect our paths to be adjacent to White people. It is our job to recognize this so that sustainable DEI[3] work can be implemented for the Classical Music field.

3 Diversity, Equity and Inclusion is an initiative that encourages representation and engagement of different groups of people (races, ethnicities, sexual orientations, genders, abilities/disabilities, ages and religions) through programs and systems.

LACK OF OPPORTUNITY
How Black Musicians Face Many Setbacks Early in Their Career as a Result of the Systemic Inequalities in the Arts

Devin Aaron Witt

Being Black in the Arts is about a **Lack of Opportunity**

It is inherently impossible to separate the ideas of being Black in the Arts and simply being Black in America. Black People and other People of Color have inherited an intentionally broken system, and those systemic faults have led us to experience many hardships that other demographics in the country don't have. Many Black families struggle to find stable housing, especially housing to purchase (rather than lease). When housing is more difficult to find, many families, like mine, have to move far more frequently than our peers, leading to more stress at school, with finding friends, and with getting established early in Arts programs. The severe underfunding of many of our school systems exacerbates this problem. This leads to underrepresentation, underperformance, and a set up towards failure. It also feeds a cycle which mirrors, but in reverse, the property tax-school performance cycle: as schools underperform more and more, families that have the means to scrape by and move to a new one do, while those who remain at the school are left with an even more underperforming school. Arts programs get cut and Black children lose another means of expressing themselves. In schools where Arts programs are still present in the higher grades (many programs are cut for older students), there are often many other issues with the school. Since there are less financial resources, there are less professional staff such as counselors, career coaches, and paraprofessionals to guide students in the right direction. Many students do not even learn about many scholarships and opportunities for higher education, because their school simply does not have the funding, resources, and time capital to distribute that information. Personally, although I tried to stay on top of as much information as possible, there were still so many opportunities that were never made known to me. The first time I took one of our nationwide standardized tests, I missed the threshold for what would've been a full tuition and fees waiver for any in-state public University. Since I was never told about that statewide scholarship, it was a missed opportunity for me to get a small leg up on my finances by not needing to work in school. Since my school only had 2 counselors for over 2,000 students, it was easy for information to 'fall through the cracks".

In many metropolitan areas, there are a number of "honor" youth ensembles, festivals, and conferences, but these events are consistently (even if unintentionally) less helpful to our Black students. These events are often in parts of town that are prohibitively far (the most prestigious honor wind ensemble in my metro area was a 1.5- hour drive through town to get to), have exorbitant fees that many Black families can not afford to pay, and have a demographic makeup that is not at all welcoming to Black students. It can be, and is, difficult to always be the only (or one of a few)

Black people in an honor ensemble. This is in the formative years of a teenager's life, when seeing representation, diversity, and inclusion are paramount to their development, self-worth, and progression. Even if all of those factors have been overcome, it is very easy for students to feel like a 'token' or just a satisfaction of some arbitrary quota. This can lead even the most steadfast of students to become discouraged and stop seeking out opportunities in honor ensembles. Music Directors are often complacent at best and blatantly discriminatory at worse—they are often more interested in the status quo. In a country where the "status quo" has involved systematic, constant, incessant, painful oppression of minorities, the status quo is harmful. There is no easy way to fix this—none at all. It takes diligent work from ensemble directors, community leaders, art advocates, and teachers to slowly reform the system — one student, one rehearsal, one step at a time.

Progressing through a Black student's journey: Once they get to college, it often gets even harder. Although the Federal Stafford loans can be a gateway into at least getting into college, since Black families often have less access to credit and "good" debt, paying for school for Black students can be tragically difficult. In many situations, Black students will need to work one or multiple jobs to pay for their school. If their school is paid for by a scholarship, there are still living costs, textbooks, transportation, and more that aren't factored in. Having access to less wealth early creates a snowball effect for Black college students, which is something I personally experienced. More difficult decisions are forced to be made than are comfortable:

Do I drop this class so I don't get an F and lose my Satisfactory Academic Progress, or do I keep it and take less hours at work and risk not paying for my car this month?

Do I double down on my coursework this semester but risk burning out and not having a fallback?

Do I go homeless this semester so I can save up to buy an introductory instrument just so I can participate in ensembles without being shamed by my peers?

When these opportunities pass, Black students are still often left with other issues relating to their academic, musical, and professional progression. As summer festivals and camps (which are still plagued by the issues mentioned before) pop up, many Black students cannot go. Sometimes the lack of ability to afford it is direct, but other times, it can be more nuanced—the University might provide a scholarship for the festival, but that is still a week or two off of work, away from the apartment, away from family, etc. That same lack of opportunity pops up time and time again and it sometimes feels like quicksand. The harder you try to get out of it, the more and more it sinks you in. When we struggle so long to just stay afloat, getting "ahead of the chains" can seem just impossible.

In the United States, and many other countries in the world, Black people are consistently at risk for lower life expectancy, more health complications, higher stress levels, and lower performance because of the higher Cortisol levels from the stress that sometimes starts as early as infancy. These issues compound on all of the other societal issues Black people deal with—which leads to not only physical health problems but mental health problems. It is hard to put into words the exact toll that feeling like an outsider at ALL TIMES can put on a person. This can funnel into depression, anxiety, and other mental health disorders. When those are stacked on top of the other issues Black people face in society, it can expound upon the disparities.

With all of these points, some experiences can still feel negatively surreal, even if a Black person has "made it" according to society. Rather than being recognized for their hard work, Black people are often told that it is a 'miracle' or 'dumb luck' that they made it out of their communities or situations. Sitting in an orchestra section where there is only one Black person, and being told that (even if presented friendly or innocently), is dehumanizing, hurtful, and by default adding to the problem rather than working to solve it. There have been numerous times where a Black artist joins an ensemble, and the conductor expects them to be an expert in Hip-Hop music, or to automatically want to perform a free concerto during February to "meet that quota." The Arts has always been rife with tokenism, and although we are moving towards inclusion, Arts organizations nationwide and worldwide have a long way to go until they are even lockstep with the minimal strides society is taking. I have personally been stopped by security at the end of a gig, asking why I'm wearing an instrument on my back after a concert. Sometimes the sheer thought of a Black person being even moderately successful is so intuitively backwards in the minds of many people, that their biases show and the arc towards anti-racism takes one step backwards.

These stories are all incredibly important. They are not told enough. Many people are keen on not learning about the challenging stories of Black people, Black Artists, Black

Brothers and Sisters, because it means that society may have to continue to work hard to confront their world views and the systems that are in place to hurt Black people. As society learns more about these stories, it will become a more welcoming and inclusive place. Not overcoming or squandering our differences, but embracing them—welcoming all of the beautiful things that make being Black wonderful, and how bringing the Black experience into our workplace as artists can make the world a more beautiful place. We, as Black people, have a beautiful, complicated, hard, nuanced, history which has a place in the Arts. Not as a token, not as a quota fulfilled, not as a statistic, but as a part of society's shared experience in its walk towards joy.

Riding the Waves of Progress

Loki Karuna

For many professionals in the Western classical arts, entering and maintaining a position in the field is the result of planning to do so through the identification of a pathway that works best. This has not been the case for the various positions that I've held in the field. For me, much of my success and upward mobility has been built on taking what I can get and creating value and opportunity out of what has been afforded to me. Where many see challenge, I see opportunity.

When life has given me lemons, I've made limoncello. When the proverbial waves of lack of privilege and economic ability have attempted to wash away my chances to exist and thrive in the field, I've ridden those waves like a skilled surfer, all the way to where I am today.

In the Beginning

While I consider the beginning of my musical training as something that happened in church as a kid, high school band actually gave me the start of my "professional" (paid) musical career. My school had an agreement with Opera Memphis (who used our facilities for rehearsals), and when on-stage "banda" members were needed for a production of La Bohéme, I was among the students selected. This was my first paid gig, and there would be several others before I graduated high school.

By the time I'd completed my 3rd year of undergraduate school, I'd won my first semi-regular orchestra job with the South Arkansas Symphony. I'd get to rehearsals and performances the best way I could (while playing on a borrowed instrument), but it was the best way that I knew how to follow my dreams while keeping having enough money to feed myself. This opportunity opened up many other doors, and served as the foundation to the next leg of my musical journey. After graduating with a Bachelor's Degree in Bassoon Performance, I moved to Los Angeles where I would earn a Master's Degree and play with several orchestras, including the Southeast Symphony, the American Youth Symphony and the Debut Orchestra. I won a fellowship with the Detroit Symphony Orchestra soon after, and from there I moved on to a tenured position with the Knoxville Symphony Orchestra, in addition to performing as a sub with the Louisville Orchestra, the Saint Paul Chamber Orchestra, and several others.

Being the only Black musician in most of the spaces I worked in was something that I never completely got used to, but leaving the profession that I worked so hard to enter was not an option; I'd worked too hard and had gotten too lucky to consider a complete change in career. So in 2016, instead of searching for work completely outside the white-centric space of "classical" music, I began shifting my career to classical radio. As my profile and unique approach to programming gained a more national spotlight, I took a job as a nationally-syndicated classical host in 2018 in my (now) home of Saint Paul, MN. In August of 2020 my Black-centered approach to programming became a cause to terminate me from my job, which allowed me to start my own business (TrillWerks Media) as an independent content creator and producer. Since then, I've been able to host and produce multiple nationally syndicated programs, including two seasons of "The Sound of 13", while engaging collaborations with countless schools, universities, conservatories, museums, and public media institutions. In June of 2022, my work caught the attention of the American Composers Orchestra, where I now serve as Director of Artist Equity, spreading my activism and advocacy into live music spaces as well as continuing to work toward the decolonization of "classical" music over digital and terrestrial broadcast airwaves.

Representation in the Field

To a degree, I feel that I represent my specific corner of the field adequately. Despite America's 2020 "racial awakening" and a renewed attention to equity in the arts, there still isn't a lot of Western classical media produced with Black musicians and consumers in mind; being among the many Black content creators who are working for change within the so-called classical music industry is an honor and I am proud to take my place in it.

When it comes to the "classical" music industry from a broader perspective, I feel very underrepresented. My definitions of classical music don't center European traditions or traditional white American senilities; the educational and professional institutions of the field operate antithetically. One of my biggest hopes is to see people like me in positions of impact at arts institutions so that the way classical music is approached and considered in the United States is actually representative of America. This is how I justify my current position with the American Composers Orchestra: it's up to me to be the change that I want to see, and being given this opportunity proves my dedication to the work.

The TRILLOQUY Podcast

In radio there's something called a "break" (the time between music where a host is talking to the audience). The way I approached my breaks was to relate the music to modern ideas and contemporary culture, instead of telling stories that are centuries old. As my audiences continued to respond to this, I decided that I wanted to expand those "breaks" into longer form content. A radio show that does this wasn't really of interest to anyone at the institution I worked for at the time, so I created TRILLOQUY to serve that purpose: expanding radio breaks that address current issues with classical music into long form, on-demand content. The official mission of TRILLOQUY is to decolonize the traditional definitions and conversations surrounding classical music. To date, the show has published over 150 episodes (or opuses, as we say), and has featured Pulitzer Prize, Emmy, and Grammy winners, along with some of the field's most progressive and forward-thinking musicians, advocates, and activists. TRILLOQUY has listenership in over 50 countries, and has pulled in revenue that has not only helped maintained myself financially, but supported 3 part-time staff members over its 3 ½ seasons.

Challenges and Barriers

I hesitate to use the word "challenge", in regard to my

work—where many see challenge, I see opportunity. With that said, there have certainly been more "opportunities" than I can name here. The biggest of them, by far, was getting fired from my radio job at Minnesota Public Radio/ American Public Media. My ideas of diverse and equitable programming didn't match theirs, which during the height of COVID, forced me into an entrepreneurial space. It's an opportunity that I didn't think that I would have to face, but one that I am grateful to have conquered. Without being pushed into the world of independent work, I wouldn't be where I am today, and certainly would not have created the public profile that's opened other professional doors for me, including my position as Director of Artist Equity with the American Composers Orchestra.

While money always offers "opportunities" for growth, time has also been something that I've had to become more intentional about rationing and utilizing. Managing a podcast with weekly guests who are professionals in the field isn't easy work; doing this while producing other projects, offering lectures and workshops, and staying on top of my bassoon playing as much as I can stacks up quickly. A portfolio style career is also the kind of work that doesn't always offer immediate benefit or gratification, but I wouldn't have it any other way.

Our ancestors faced challenges that we could never imagine - enslavement, Black codes, Jim Crow, etc. Challenge is a part of life, especially for Black people. But identifying those challenges as opportunities is the greater aspect of our collective struggle.

Great Privilege and Great Responsibility

Responsibility is the exact word I use when it comes to who and what I feature and center in my work. I am grateful to have a strong team and strong body of supporters who help facilitate my work. I've remained consistent in my brand and mission; most of my TRILLOQUY guests are Black, POC and gender-marginalized artists. And those who are not are always prepared to advocate for minority artists as well.

The Degree of Progress, So Far

The field of classical radio and content creation needs an overhaul – as it currently stands I would give our field a D+. While classical and public radio has done a phenomenal job of hiring and platforming women and queer artists, Black people (who reject respectability politics, in particular) are still being left out of the decision making.

The first thing that I think should be done is to incentivize diverse hiring – any "classical" institution whose staff is more than 60% white should lose their tax-deductible/non-profit status. We must force diversity, and more specifically, BLACKNESS, into American arts institutions. The way I decenter and critique the traditions of our field manifest in various ways, but remains the centrepin of my overall mission.

Staying in the Fight

My biggest motivation toward maintaining a position in the field of "classical" music is opportunity. I've been given the talents, the platforms and the community to do a unique style of work focused on radical change. It's my responsibility to take on the opportunity every day in every way I can.

Among my many mentors is Daisaku Ikeda, President of the Soka Gakkai, which is a Buddhist organization that I joined in late 2020. His mantra is "Never Give Up".

I hold this, alongside the struggles of Afro-Americans over the generations close to my heart and will continue to push forward in every way that I can toward the ultimate (and in my view, inevitable) decolonization of classical music in America.

About the Contributors

Each contributor of this Volume of From Our Eyes & Ears is a current or past music student, educator, performer, administrator, and/or activist of Black descent. They are colleagues, mentors, and friends who I have met throughout my education and professional endeavors. Their perspectives along with the perspectives of many other people of color show the need for radical change within our field of western "classical" music.

To the contributors, thank you for being a part of this journey.

Much Love,
Lorin

A proud native of Memphis, TN, **Loki Karuna** (formerly Garrett McQueen) is a bassoonist who has performed with ensembles including the South Arkansas Symphony, Jackson Symphony, American Youth Symphony, Memphis Repertory Orchestra, the Eroica Ensemble, and the Knoxville Symphony Orchestra, the Sphinx Symphony Orchestra, Memphis Symphony Orchestra, the Southeast Symphony, the Artosphere and Gateways Festival Orchestras, the St. Paul Chamber Orchestra, the Louisville Orchestra, and the Detroit Symphony Orchestra. Loki has been featured as both a performer and host on "Performance Today" and "Music Through the Night" from American Public Media, and has appeared in a wide array of television programs, including Oxygen's "Snapped: Killer Couples", TV One's "Fatal Attraction", and Fox's "Glee".

In addition to remaining active in performance spaces, Loki is the host and producer of local and nationally-syndicated radio programs including "The Sound of 13", "Noteworthy", "Gateways Radio", and "The Sounds of Kwanzaa". Away from the airwaves, Loki offers guest lectures, presentations, and trainings at the intersections of race, culture, Black liberation, and classical music, with past collaborators including the Gateways Music Festival, the Sphinx Organization, the Kennedy Center, the Apollo Theater, Black Music Experience, the Minnesota Music Teachers Association, New Music Gathering, and the MacPhail Center for Music. In the press, Loki has been noted as not only a "classical agitator", but also "a Black talent in public media that you may not know, but should". In 2021, the New York Times noted his weekly podcast, TRILLOQUY, as a standout and one that is "required listening for industry leaders and listeners alike."

Loki holds a Bachelor of Music in Bassoon Performance from the University of Memphis, where he studied with Lecolion Washington, and a Master of Music in Bassoon Performance from the University of Southern California, where he studied with Judith Farmer. Alongside working as a performer, the Executive Producer and co-host of the TRILLOQUY podcast and President of TrillWerks Media, Loki is the Director of Artist Equity for the American Composers Orchestra. He serves on the board of directors for the American Composers Forum, the Beethoven Festival Orchestra, Lyrica Baroque, and the Cedar Cultural Center, and maintains leadership and artistic advisory positions with the Black Opera Alliance, the Gateways Music Festival, and the Lakes Area Music Festival.

Loki is a practitioner of Nichiren Buddhism, leading the Summit Hill district of Soka Gakkai International, and spends his free time studying Eastern philosophy, eating plant-based cuisine, and enjoying life with his partner, Dell.

Jammie Phillips has worked in music education for over 15 years. New to the state of Alabama from Georgia, she is currently the band director at McKee Middle School in Montgomery, AL. Phillips has built a career delivering consecutive Superior & Excellent ratings for her band programs in Georgia and now Alabama. She is a graduate of Bethune-Cookman University with a degree in Music Education, and she has also obtained graduate degrees in Education & Administrator Leadership. Mrs. Phillips was recently selected to be a National Teacher Leader for the National Association for Music Education (NAFME), as well as a 2022 Golden Anniversary Award winner for The National Flute Association (NFA). Mrs. Phillips is a freelance Flutist and Mother of 3. Some of her organizations include Sigma Alpha Iota International Music Fraternity, as well as Zeta Phi Beta Sorority, Inc.

Stephanie N Phillips born January 12th, is a Native and Black American woman. She is originally from Augusta, Ga and graduated from Davidson Fine Arts magnet school as well as Augusta University with a bachelor's degree in classical percussion. She is a musician who plays percussion, drum set and piano as well. She currently resides in Philadelphia, Pa where she graduated from Temple University with her masters in Music Performance. She enjoys the different aspects of music including performing, writing, creating, producing and business. One of her goals in life was to become an educator and she currently is serving as a music teacher in the Philadelphia public school system.

Nasia Shearod is a graduate of Kennesaw State University, where she earned her Bachelors of Arts in Music Education with a focus in Choral Education. Post-graduation, she taught several private students, pursuing her desire to inspire young musicians to mindful wellness that music brings. She then transitioned into the role of Enrollment Specialist at Benalytics Consulting Group LLC., where she assisted individuals in enrolling in health coverage at the Federal Health Insurance Marketplace, Medicare, and Medicaid. It was there that she rediscovered her passion for cultivating safe and constant communities and opportunities for marginalized individuals and groups. Her philosophy is that all are deserving of whole wellness- the key to leading a fulfilled and sustainable life- and that aid and support can be accessible for all. She currently works alongside financial advisors at 1847 Financial (formerly called Penn Mutual) as the Recruiting Coordinator. Her other passions include music, education, reading as many books as possible, crafting, writing, and being the best dog mom she can be.

Dr. Arris Golden (she/her) is the Assistant Director of Bands and Associate Drector of the Spartan Marching Band at Michigan State University. In this capacity, Dr. Golden teaches courses in conducting, marching band techniques, conducts the Spartan Youth Wind Symphony, is coordinator of the MSU Performing Arts Camps, and assists with all aspects of the athletic band program. Before joining the faculty at Michigan State University, Dr. Golden was a member of the conducting faculty at the University of North Carolina at Chapel Hill, where she served as the Assistant Director of University Bands.

Prior to her collegiate appointments, Dr. Golden had a distinguished 18-year teaching career in the public schools of North Carolina. In her last public school assignment, Dr. Golden conducted the premiere of four commissioned works that have become standards in the middle school band repertoire: "Kitsune: The Fox Spirits," by Brian Balmages (2009), "The Machine Awakes" for young band and electronics by Steven Bryant (2012), "Freight Train," by Pierre LaPlante (2013), and "The Cave Your Fear" by Michael Markowski (2014).

Dr. Golden maintains an active schedule with engagements throughout the United States and internationally as a guest conductor, clinician, and adjudicator. Dr. Golden has also shared presentations at the Midwest Band and Orchestra Clinic, Michigan Music Conference, the North Carolina Music Educators Conference, and the Virginia Music Educators Conference based in her research interests: undergraduate music education preparation, conductor decision-making, repertoire selection and programming, and the student teaching and mentorship experience. Dr. Golden has worked with a number of notable composers in the preparation and performance of their works for the wind band medium. Recent and future artistic collaborations include Brian Balmages, David Biedenbender, Tyler S. Grant, Peter Meechan, Aaron Perinne, Alex Shapiro, Erika Svanoe, and Omar Thomas. Dr. Golden's professional affiliations include the College Band Directors National Association and the National Band Association; she also serves on Board of Directors of National Band Association and as a Co-Chairperson of the National Band Association's IDEA Committee.

Dr. Golden holds degrees from the University of North Carolina at Chapel Hill and the University of North Carolina at Greensboro. She completed the Doctor of Musical Arts in wind conducting from Michigan State University as a 2014 recipient of a Michigan State University Distinguished Fellowship.

Anthony Morris (he/him) is currently pursuing a Master of Music in Wind Conducting at the University of Georgia where he studies with Dr. Nicholas Williams and Dr. Jaclyn Hartenberger and serves as a Master's Conducting Associate for the UGA Bands. Mr. Morris received a Bachelor of Music in Music Education with a dual concentration in Instrumental and Choral education with Cum Laude distinction from Kennesaw State University. Prior to graduate study, Mr. Morris served as the Director of Bands & Choirs at Wildwood Middle High School where he was responsible for the instruction and administration of the middle & high school concert bands, marching band, music theory, and choir program.

Mr. Morris has appeared as a guest conductor with the United States Army Band "Pershing's Own" and was named a Conducting Fellow for the H. Robert Reynolds Conducting Institute at the 76th Annual Midwest Clinic in Chicago, Illinois. His passion for music education has led him to create the Relative Pitch Podcast which discusses modern issues regarding music education and helps pave the way for much-needed change to make a more diverse, enriching, and equitable music community. Through these endeavors, Mr. Morris and Relative Pitch Podcast presented sessions entitled "Changing of the Guard: Shifting Perspectives of Education" at the College Band Directors National Association National Conference and "Pushing for Change From the Inside: Bringing Equity to Middle and High School Bands" at the annual Georgia Music Educators Association In-Service Conference.

Professional affiliations include Collegiate Band Directors National Association, National Association for Music Educators, Georgia Music Educator Association, Florida Music Educator Association, Florida Bandmasters Association, and Phi Mu Alpha Sinfonia.

Having a passion for youth and community engagement, **Nicholas Felder** (he/him) creates art that inspires relational bonds between people in a given space. He builds community in artmaking, unlocking truths around self-identity, and creating a space for embodied expression.

Nicholas has taught and led arts programs with the Neutral Zone (Ann Arbor, MI), Detroit Symphony Orchestra, and American Composers Orchestra. He loves to encourage teens to express their social and political views through artmaking.

In addition to composing and performing, Nicholas is an active creative writer and has authored numerous poems and short stories about identity, Blackness, sexuality, love and belonging. His work *My Little Texas* (2021) details his upbringing and growing relationship with love, living in Houston. Selections of the work are featured in *Fifth Wall* Performing Arts' Black Hearts, Black Voices II album.

Nicholas loves freshly brewed coffee, any kind of earthy color (probably because he's a Taurus) and laughing out loud with his friends and family. For more on Nicholas, find him at https://www.nicholasfelder.com/

Marcel Benoit (he/him) is a young professional, born and raised in Atlanta.

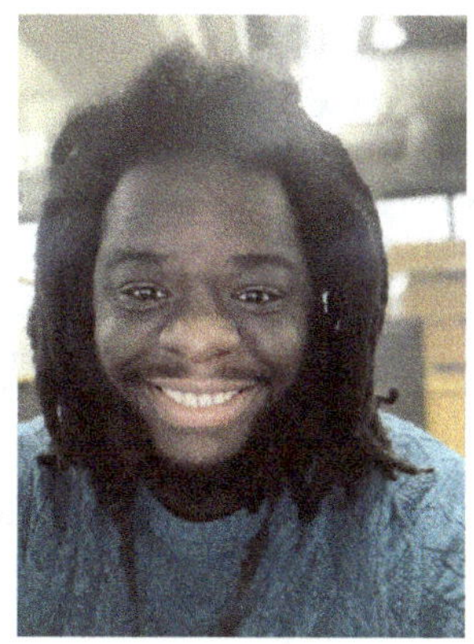

"I'm a classically trained Baritone vocalist and have been singing my entire life. Music has been an integral part of my development and it fills me with joy to incorporate it in my daily life. My contribution to this text comes from the prejudice that I have experienced in the past as well as the discrimination I avoid to this day. My hope is that the words of my colleagues and I might reach the right people to make a difference in our society. Our understanding of music will always be corrupt, if we don't make an effort to make our voices heard."

Camille Core (she/her) is from Douglasville, Ga. She is a classically trained soprano who studied under renowned tenor Todd Wedge. She served as the secretary for the Kennesaw State University chapter of the Collegiate National Association for Music Educators. She also served on the executive board for the Black Musicians Coalition as treasurer and secretary respectively. She graduated from Kennesaw State University in 2023 with a Bachelor's Degree in Music Education with a choral specification.She is currently a choral director in Cherokee County, GA.

Alissa Gittens (she/her) attended Morgan State University where she studied with Dr. Anita Thesen and performed with various ensembles before receiving her Bachelor of Arts Degree of Music in 2005. Currently, she works as the Communications Manager for the Arts Education in Maryland Schools, teaches flute privately, and proudly serves as a Performing and Fine Arts Recruiting Consultant for her alma mater. In the fall of 2020, Alissa launched the Urban Flautistas Fest, a platform for flutists of color to present their work and build community. In her efforts to promote BIPOC representation in music education, Ms. Gittens became an official ambassador for Nuvo Flutes in 2018 and joined the Association of Black Women Band Directors as an associate member in 2020. Past positions include her work as the Director of Programs for The MusicianShip, a non-profit organization in Washington D.C. that provides music instruction support to schools and community based music programs.

Alissa finds great joy in working with young musicians. She has served as a flute adjudicator for the Prince Georges County Schools District Solo and Ensemble Music Festival and clinician for the Reid Temple Youth Orchestra Workshops. In addition, she provides flute clinics in schools throughout the East coast and has presented masterclasses at the University of the West Indies and the University of the Southern Caribbean on the island of Trinidad and Tobago. Her ensemble affiliations include the Reid Temple AME Church Orchestra, Fort Washington Symphonic Winds, Howard County Ballet Orchestra, Go-Go Symphony, and as the founder of Anita's Flutes Choir.

In addition to her love of music, Alissa is passionate about social justice. Her life goal includes (1) opening music outreach centers in communities where opportunities for music education are under-resourced and (2) developing instrumental music conferences dedicated to promoting artistic exchange between the African Diaspora within the Americas and the Caribbean. It is her belief that music is a powerful tool for social change.

Ashley Michelle Crawford was born in Memphis, Tn into a life of music. From the sounds of her own father, Hubert "H-Bomb" Crawford, grandfather, Hubert Crawford, Sr. of "Hubert Crawford and The King Riders Band," older brother and accomplished producer and bassist, Anthony Crawford, and cousin, Hank Crawford, legendary saxophonist, she was destined to pave her path in the field of music. She began playing flute at age 11 and has used her gift as a pathway to musical performance, education, and opportunities. Ashley received her Bachelor's degree from Tennessee State University where she studied under retired professor, Belinda Laupp and marched in the world renowned, "Aristocrat of Bands" and served as piccolo section leader in 2010. During her studies at TSU she was rewarded a full music scholarship, the "Director's Choice Award" and "Best Section." She also studied the origins of instrumental music abroad in Vienna, Austria and Florence, Italy. She went on to complete her master's in Instrumental Pedagogy and Classical Flute Performance at Belmont University in 2014. While at BU, she studied under Dr. Carolyn Totaro, became a 2x concerto competition winner, was a music scholarship recipient, winner of the "Friends of the Arts President's Choice Award," and published two theses, "An investigation of four works for flute." and "The causes, prevention, and treatment of flute-playing related injury and pain." Her classical training also includes masterclass study from renowned flutists, Dr. Yvonne Chavez Hansbrough, Mark Vinci, Rhonda Larson, and Dr. Nicole Riner at Skidmore College in Saratoga Springs, NY.

Ashley Crawford has expanded her outreach of music education by being a visiting music tutor in the Metro Nashville Public School and Shelby County School districts. She has coached and privately taught at Hunter's Lane High School, Whitehaven High School, East Nashville Magnet Middlle/High School, H.G Hill Middle School, Jere Baxter Middle School, Cane Ridge High School, Rose Parks Math/Science Magnet School, and Thurgood Marshall Middle School. She has also been the flute instructor at summer band camp and intensives, Nashville Fine Arts Academy and Edward L. Graves summer band camp. Her career in pedagogy came full circle when she became the Flute Professor at Tennessee State University where she currently teaches applied flute, flute choir, and heads the woodwind area of the music department. She also leads a community group, the "Nashville Philharmonic Flute Ensemble," as their conductor and musical director and serves as President of the Nashville African American Wind Symphony, Inc. As a result of her community work and outreach, she was recognized in Belmont University's 2022 Top 100 Entrepreneur Awards. Ashley also appeared as a guest conductor for the Mid-south flute Society's Collegiate Flute Choir and adjudicator for the Music Teacher National Association's Young Artist Competition. She has also appeared and performed as a guest clinician for the National Flute Association, Umoja Flute Institute, and Midwest Clinic International Band and Orchestra Conference.

Ashley has dedicated her life to sharing her gift and knowledge of flute to people of all ages. Her trademarked brand, "Flutebae" was birthed after her 2017 viral sensation video of the #MaskOffChallenge. Ever since, she has fused the sounds of classical flute with the latest Hip-Hop, Pop, and R&B music that has helped propel flute into mainstream music and media. She has appeared under her entity, "FluteBae," at the Staples Center with her rendition of the National Anthem for the NBA LA Lakers and WNBA LA Sparks. She has collaborated with prominent artists and producers such as Chris Hines, David "SkiBeatz" Willis, Gaither Vocal Band, Soul Sessions, Sir The Baptist, Dubba-AA, and Brassville. She has curated virtual performances such as "We. Will. Breathe." by FluteBae, that raised awareness for Black Lives Matter and hope in the black community and allies to keep fighting for equality. This performance rewarded her the opportunity to appear in flute publication, "The Flute View" with an artist interview. She also appears in the "Flute Examiner," the 2023 "People Issue" of the Nashville Scene, Nashville's "Urbannite", NPR, WPLN, and as a featured artist on grammy-award winning "Best Roots Gospel" album, "The Urban Hymnal," by the Aristocrat of Bands. Ashley "FluteBae" Crawford prides herself on being a teaching-artist who uses education and creativity to reach the masses and encourage people to embrace learning and performing music. She embodies the element of flute through her sultry and robust playing, bridging the gap between pop culture and classical music. Her melodious tone sings effortlessly and is felt on a visceral level. There are no limits to her style and her playing transcends all genres.

A passionate collaborator and advocate for diversity in the arts, **Camille Jones** has worked with various festival orchestras and chamber groups, including the National Orchestral Institute and Festival (NOI + F), Bowdoin International Music Festival, and Next Festival of Emerging Artists.

As a 2019 Sphinx Orchestral Futurist Fellow, she has helped commission works and curate a professional development workshop for K-12 students in Prince George's County, Maryland. This project piloted what is now the K12 New Music Initiative, a commissioning project to expand the repertoire of K12 orchestras with music by BIPOC composers. In the Fall of 2018, she curated Voices Unheard, a concert series at UMD that celebrated works by women composers and composers of color. In addition, she had the opportunity to collaborate with esteemed cello professor Anthony Elliott for a concert series at the Kerrytown Concerthouse titled Passing the Torch in 2021 and 2022. Camille is establishing herself as a freelance artist in the Michigan area as well, having performed for singer Michael Bublé, rapper Big Sean and Darren Criss. She has also served as a teaching artist for the Detroit Symphony Orchestra's Civic Youth Ensembles as well as the Sphinx Overture program in Detroit. Camille currently serves as the African-American fellow for the Virginia Symphony Orchestra for their 23/24 season.

Camille received her B.M. in Violin Performance at the University of Maryland, College Park and a M.M. in Violin Performance from the University of Michigan, having studied under Danielle Belen.

Andrew Wynn (b. 2000) is a native to Olney, Illinois. After completing high school in Ardmore, Alabama, he moved to Kennesaw, Georgia to pursue his BA in Music Performance on the trumpet. At the same time, he enlisted into the Georgia Army National Guard as a bandsman and is currently a Sergeant in the 116 th Army Band, based out of Dobbins Air Reserve Base, where he keeps a very active schedule of performing for audiences all around the state of Georgia. After two years as a music student, he switched his focus to writing and is currently and English Major at Kennesaw State University. As an English major, he has done extensive research into African American English and Hawaiian Pidgin, to educate others on the historical and present implications of systemic racism. SGT Wynn will soon be transitioning to the Active Duty Component of the U.S. Army to continue his career as an actively-performing musician.

Dr. Tonya Mitchell-Spradlin is Director of Wind Band Studies and Assistant Professor of Music at Penn State University. In addition to conducting the Symphonic Wind Ensemble, overseeing the graduate wind conducting program, teaching courses in wind band literature and wind conducting, she oversees all aspects of the concert bands at Penn State. Her appointment at PSU follows three years as Assistant Director of Bands and Associate Director of Athletic Bands at the University of South Carolina. Prior to her time at UofSC, Mitchell-Spradlin taught at Valdosta State University as Director of Athletic Bands, and was Director of Bands at Chamblee High School in Chamblee, Georgia for four years.

Mitchell-Spradlin has a diverse background as a conductor, clinician, adjudicator, educator, and speaker. She is a Conn Selmer educator and frequent guest conductor with performances with several regional honor bands, Allstate bands, summer camps and clinics, and residencies at public schools and collegiate institutions. She is active in the teaching of conducting having served as clinician for the UMKC Conducting Symposium and the President's Own Marine Band Conductor Training Program.

As a presenter, Mitchell-Spradlin speaks often about programming, forming a connection with musicians, building culture, musical leadership, and inclusivity in the band medium. She has shared musical and pedagogical ideas on several music podcasts including Everything Band, Conn Selmer's Backstage with Dr. Tim, The Bandroom, and the Ictus Podcast. Presentations include invited sessions at the Midwest Band and Orchestra Clinic, College Music Society, the College Band Directors National Association, SCMEA, KMEA, NYSBDA, and keynote presenter for the NAfME Northwest conference. Her international speaking engagements include presenting the keynote for the Maryborough Music Conference in Australia and a session on Joan Tower's Fanfares for the Uncommon Woman for the International Society for the Advancement and Promotion of Wind Band Society (IGEB) in Oberwölz, Austria. A proponent for advancing the wind ensemble medium, she led the consortium and premiere of Aaron Perrine's *Beneath a Canvas of Green* for wind ensemble and percussion quartet which was also the source of her doctoral dissertation. Additionally, she is active in a number of premieres and consortiums for new music.

Under her direction, the Penn State Symphonic Wind Ensemble has received several honors including a performance at the prestigious Heinz Hall in Pittsburgh, PA as part of Penn State's President's Concert as well as an invitation to perform at the College Band Directors National Association Eastern Region Conference in Ithaca, New York. The ensemble has recorded *The Hardscrabble* by Steven Rice for wind ensemble and 12+ double reeds for release on Neuma Records as well as Evan Ziporyn's *Impulse Control* - concerto for drumset and wind ensemble for release on Parma Records.

Mitchell-Spradlin served as the National Vice President of Professional Relations for Tau Beta Sigma: National Honorary Band Sorority for two years. She serves on the National Band Association Selective Music List Committee, the College Band Directors National Association Diversity Committee, and also holds memberships in the College Band Directors National Association, College Music Society, PMEA, National Association for Music Education, Black Women Band Directors Association, and Women Band Directors International.

Robyn Smith is the newly appointed Principal Trombonist of the Chicago Sinfonietta Orchestra and former Second Trombonist of the Detroit Opera. Robyn graduated with a Master of Music from the New England Conservatory studying under the tutelage of Toby Oft, principal trombone of the Boston Symphony. In her most recent engagements,

Robyn has played, as a substitute, with the St. Louis Symphony, The Boston Pops and has toured internationally with the Boston Symphony. She has also previously performed as a fellow with the Tanglewood Music Center Orchestra, The New World Symphony, National Repertory Orchestra, American Repertory Theatre, Dee Dee Bridgewater Big Band at the Detroit Jazz Festival and with the artist Lizzo at the 62nd Annual Grammy Awards. She performs with a variety of ensembles and is an associate artist with the Rodney Marsalis Big Brass. Robyn's solo work includes a performance at Michigan State University's MLK tribute concert and as a featured soloist on New England Conservatory's Contemporary Ensemble concert. Her awards extend internationally as she was the winner of the 2018 International Trombone Association's Marsteller Solo Competition. Robyn is an advocate for the dismantling of oppressive structures that contribute to the lack of black and brown faces within high art forms. She teaches privately while also teaching through the Sistema Ravinia program that targets underrepresented youth in music. Robyn also mentors young black and brown musicians with goals of becoming professional musicians in various programs across the country.

Devin Witt, low brass artist and native of Atlanta, Georgia, is an active freelancer, contractor, and music services provider, holding versatility and the relentless pursuit of musical mastery as his core values.

Mr. Witt serves as the trombonist, horn arranger, and as a producer for Steel Toe Stiletto, one of the leading corporate bands in the country. He is also the director and Arranger of the 10 piece Imagine Brass Band. Mr. Witt is also a member of the Atlanta Latin Jazz Orchestra, an 18-piece latin big band under the direction of Mr. Rob Opitz. Additionally, Mr. Witt is a member of the Neo-Jazz Fusion group Rebel Big Band and can be heard on their recent eponymous EP.

Mr. Witt is active in the Atlanta Musical Theatre scene, having performed at the Fox theater, City Springs Theater Company, the Alliance Theater, and more. He also serves as a consultant for local schools to add live music and technology to their productions.

He is equally comfortable performing in symphony orchestras as big bands, and every genre in between, including funk, party bands, chamber music, religious music, and many more. Mr. Witt is adept on all low brass instruments, including the entire trombone family, euphonium, tuba, sousaphone, and bass trumpet.

His primary teachers have included Brian Hecht, Dr. Tom Gibson, Sam Skelton, Nathan Zgonc, and Wes Funderburk.

Mr. Witt graduated from Kennesaw State University with a Bachelor's of Music in Music Performance.

Jessica Bell is a highly skilled and enthusiastic clarinetist with a passion for teaching, woodworking, instrument repair, and research as it relates to the clarinet. Jessica, a passionate music enthusiast, embarked on a remarkable journey of research in Tanzania. Combining her love for music and environmental conservation, she delved into the world of mpingo conservation—a wood used to craft clarinets. Through her meticulous research, Jessica aimed to understand the impact of mpingo harvesting on the local ecosystem and the role clarinet-making plays in sustaining both cultural heritage and environmental stewardship. She has taken her findings to national research stages and most recently internationally, winning the International Clarinet Association Research Competition and publication in the Clarinet Journal. With a solid foundation in instrument repair, Jessica has honed her skills through extensive work at Southeast Music Institute. She has worked with an impressive range of instruments from Yamaha to Buffet Crampon to vintage metal clarinets. Jessica's approach to her craft is rooted in clarity, which drives her to constantly research and develop her skills. She believes in reaching the highest standards and strives to innovate all aspects of the clarinet experience while holding on to the industry's traditions. Jessica has been teaching private clarinet lessons for 8 years and has created a growing community (Comprehensive Clarity) on YouTube. Sustainability is a big concern for Jessica as she continues to research current materials used for aspects of clarinet production and potential new materials that could be used.

Wendy Caudle is a classically trained oboist and singer with a love of many genres of music ranging from Gregorian Chant to Hip-Hop and Rap. In her 20-plus year music career, Ms. Caudle has been a band director, choir director, adjunct music faculty, church musician, freelance performer and a private instructor, but it was her work in music education that compelled her to become an advocate for students experiencing bias, microaggressions, discrimination and stereotyping.

Propelled by her own personal experiences with racism (particularly in the field of classical music), her desire to advocate for and protect students and her knowledge of the way the public school system is built and runs, Ms. Caudle began working to disrupt and dismantle systemic racism in her public school system and greater community.

Partnering with parents, community organizations, elected officials and community leaders Ms. Caudle focused on closing the opportunity gap, ensuring access to rigorous academics for underrepresented populations, securing mental health support for students of color experiencing racial trauma, and discipline disproportionality. This led to the school system creating an Equity Department which provided mandatory DEI professional development for teachers, a curriculum review to ensure the contributions of all groups were included in history, english, math & science and fine arts, an audit and revision of hiring practices, an audit and revision of acceptance criteria into magnet, gifted and AP programs, a shift from traditional discipline practices to restorative justice practices and free mental health services for students experiencing racial trauma.

But she didn't stop there. Her passion to make an impact in social justice led to a career switch. Ms. Caudle now works in local government where she advocates for citizens, offers education and enrichment opportunities, oversees governmental transparency and ensures best practices. She still maintains a private studio, sits on the board of several local arts councils and is active with her school system's fine arts department. Ms. Caudle holds a Bachelor of Arts in Music from the University of Alabama, a Master of Music from the University of

Maryland at College Park and her major teachers include the late David Weber and Ray Still.

Sydnee Goode, a Georgia native, is a recent graduate of Kennesaw State University with a degree in Choral Music Education. During her time at KSU, she made a significant impact on the campus community through the foundation and leadership of the award-winning Black Musicians Coalition, a Black organization for Black musicians created by Black musicians. This group produced The Blueprint, the first award-winning interdisciplinary Black History Production on Kennesaw campus. In addition, she served as a Student Diversity Ambassador for the Division of Diverse and Inclusive Excellence and a Student Representative for The College of the Arts Diversity, Equity, and Inclusion Committee. At the end of her junior year, Sydnee was awarded the R.O.H. Social Justice Award for Racial and Ethnic Diversity. During her senior year, she was a contributing writer for Her Campus, the leading media platform dedicated to empowering college women around the world. In the future, Sydnee plans on teaching high school choir and hopes to continue her education to become a Collegiate Choral Director. If possible, she hopes she can travel the world to teach and inspire others about the importance of music and why representation in the classroom matters.

Jeremiah Robinson is a singer, educator, and performer in the Atlanta area. Originally from Cartersville, GA, he grew up very active in his local chorus and theatre community. Robinson graduated from Kennesaw State University with a BM in Choral Music Education in 2020. Robinson is in his third year teaching and is currently holding a position at Ridgeview Charter Middle School. When he is not teaching, he can be heard performing with the Orpheus Men's Ensemble or Coro

Vocati or can catch him performing in or directing musicals throughout Atlanta.

Nassar Edwards is the orchestra director at Smith Middle School in Cypress, TX. He has studied violin under Helen Kim, a Juilliard graduate and Kenn Wagner (Atlanta Symphony Orchestra). Nassar has been a violin clinician at various schools in the Cypress, TX area and in the metro-Atlanta area during his collegiate years. Nassar served as the president of the Collegiate National Association For Music Education and American String Teachers Association at Kennesaw State University. Nassar also served as a teacher for the KSU String Project for three years. He also was the Librarian for Kennesaw State University Symphony and Philharmonic Orchestra. Nassar is a member of the American String Teachers Association and Texas Music Educators Association. Since middle school, Nassar always knew he wanted to be a music educator. Nassar enjoys listening to music and podcasts, hanging out with his friends, trying new restaurants, and hopes to influence a community through his love for music.

Recognized for her poised stage presence and rich, warm tone, **Lauryn Davis** has become a notable emerging soprano. Her recent performance highlights include operatic and music theatre roles such as Musetta in Puccini's *La bohème* and Margaret in Adam Guettel's *The Light in the Piazza*. She has been included in masterclasses with world-renowned musicians and conductors such as Pierre Vallet, Jennifer Larmore, and Chuck Hudson. In 2022 she was the winner of the Atlanta Opera Guild's Scholarship Competition, receiving the Tommy Trotter Award. Originally from Atlanta, Georgia, Lauryn is currently pursuing a Master of Music degree at the Cincinnati College-Conservatory of Music (CCM). Lauryn is a wonderful musician who plans to further her operatic career by continuing her training with other professionals at summer programs and fellowships around the world.

Alissa Gittens (she/her) attended Morgan State University where she studied with Dr. Anita Thesen and performed with various ensembles before receiving her Bachelor of Arts Degree of Music in 2005. Currently, she works as the Communications Manager for Arts Education in Maryland Schools, teaches flute privately, and proudly serves as a Performing and Fine Arts Recruiting Consultant for her alma mater. In the fall of 2020, Alissa launched the Urban Flautistas Fest, a platform for flutists of color to present their work and build community. In her efforts to promote BIPOC representation in music education, Ms. Gittens became an official ambassador for Nuvo Flutes in 2018 and joined the Association of Black Women Band Directors as an associate member in 2020. Past positions include her work as the Director of Programs for The MusicianShip, a non-profit organization in Washington D.C. that provides music instruction support to schools and community based music programs.

Alissa finds great joy in working with young musicians. She has served as a flute adjudicator for the Prince Georges County Schools District Solo and Ensemble Music Festival and clinician for the Reid Temple Youth Orchestra Workshops. In addition, she provides flute clinics in schools throughout the East coast and has presented masterclasses at the University of the West Indies and the University of the Southern Caribbean on the island of Trinidad and Tobago. Her ensemble affiliations include the Reid Temple AME Church Orchestra, Fort Washington Symphonic Winds, Howard County Ballet Orchestra, Go-Go Symphony, and as the founder of Anita's Flutes (flute choir).

In addition to her love of music, Alissa is passionate about social justice. Her life goal includes (1) opening music outreach centers in communities where opportunities for music education are under-resourced and (2) developing instrumental music conferences dedicated to promoting artistic exchange between the African Diaspora within the Americas and the Caribbean. It is her belief that music is a powerful tool for social change.

www.ingramcontent.com/pod-product-compliance
Lightning Source LLC
Chambersburg PA
CBHW061218210726
48294CB00006B/1879

* 9 7 8 1 7 3 3 0 8 9 8 6 9 *